250

THE STRUGGLE FOR THE
THIRD WORLD

The Struggle for the Third World

A BACKGROUND BOOK

Brian Crozier

THE BODLEY HEAD
LONDON

27922

© Brian Crozier 1966
Printed and bound in Great Britain for
The Bodley Head Ltd
10 Earlham Street, London, WC2
by William Clowes & Sons Ltd, Beccles
Set in Monotype Plantin
First published in 1966

CONTENTS

AUTHOR'S NOTE

HISTORY is happening too fast for comfort, and this is especially true of the countries collectively known as the 'Third World'. The term itself reflects the speed of contemporary change and means different things to different men. The French launched it as *le tiers monde*, which the Larousse defines as 'economically underdeveloped countries that belong neither to the group of States of liberal economy nor to the group of States of the socialist type'.

But the term has been used of *all* underdeveloped countries, including some communist ones, and of the uncommitted countries of Africa and Asia that have tried to keep out of military alliances with the rival power blocs.

Here again, history is playing havoc with definitions, for there are now two kinds of uncommitted countries: those that are uncommitted between the western and communist alliances, and those that try to keep equidistant from Moscow and Peking. Moreover, the Third World can no longer be limited to Africa and Asia, for the claims of Latin America to be included in it are too strong to be ignored.

All this confusion encourages me to make my own definition. For the purposes of this book, then, the Third World refers to the non-communist countries of Asia, Africa and Latin America, whether or not they have military arrangements with western nations. This is arbitrary but, I hope, clear. By this definition, Cuba, for instance, belonged to the Third World until Fidel Castro belatedly discovered that he was a communist. By the same token, countries whose governments are hostile to the West but do not so far call themselves communist —such as the United Arab Republic or Indonesia—are still

7

part of the Third World; but so is Siam, which is a leading member of the military alliance known as SEATO.

The pace of history, which has created the concept of a Third World and modified it, has also made this book necessary. In *The Rebels* (1960) I dealt with the insurrectionary movements that preceded independence in the Third World; and in *The Morning After* (1963), with the headaches independence brought. In an earlier book in the present series— *Neo-Colonialism* (1964)—I looked at the theory that the ex-imperial powers were trying to maintain their grip on their former colonies by economic and other means, and found it wanting. I now look at a much more dangerous and insidious threat to the Third World, which comes from Moscow, Peking and other communist capitals. This threat already existed in the days when communism was a monolith: it has been intensified, not reduced or removed, by the rivalry between Moscow and Peking. This, as we shall see, is the true meaning of 'the struggle for the Third World'.*

* Passages from an article of mine, which appeared under this title in the July 1964 issue of the London quarterly *International Affairs*, are incorporated in this book.

I

The Sino-Soviet Split

I

Mr Nan's Duty

―――――

'WE HAVE ALWAYS', said Mr Nan, 'considered it merely our internationalist duty to give support to the fighting Afro-Asian peoples.' The speaker, to give him his full name, was Mr Nan Han-chen. The occasion was an Afro-Asian economic seminar, the place Algiers, and the date February 23, 1965. The title of his address was at least as interesting as the words I have quoted—and longer:

'Let us Resolutely Struggle Against Imperialism and Neo-Colonialism and for the Economic Emancipation of the Afro-Asian Peoples.'

A few words of explanation seem necessary. First, the man himself. Mr Nan is an old man, as are most of the top Chinese communist leaders who, with few exceptions, have stuck together with remarkable cohesiveness since their early days of agitation in the 1920s. He was about 73 when he made his Algiers speech—a year older than the supreme leader, Mao Tse-tung. But age does not seem to have mellowed these fire-breathing Chinese leaders. Their speeches are full of references to 'fighting' and 'struggle' and, in their militancy, they have poured scorn on the revisionist Russians whom they have found guilty, among other heinous crimes, of trying to reach an understanding with America and sparing the world the horrors of a nuclear war.

A married man with a large family, Mr Nan is an economic and financial expert. This sounds mild, dry and reassuring, but words and functions have different meanings in communist societies from those that are accepted elsewhere. In Marxist terms, every activity is a struggle, especially in the Chinese People's Republic. Workers, for instance, are not called upon merely to produce more coal, or steel, or tractors, but to 'struggle to increase production', or better still, to 'win the battle to produce more' tractors, steel or coal.

Similarly, finance or economics, which we who live in non-communist societies think of as technical matters—liable, certainly, to bring experts to blows, but hardly lethal—are weapons of war to communist officials. The war in which these weapons are used is a permanent one, whether or not shots happen to be fired. It embraces the class struggle, which has an international as well as a national dimension.

On the national scale, the workers are supposed to hate the capitalists and struggle against them. Internationally, 'oppressed' countries are supposed to struggle against 'imperialist' ones. We are familiar with this phenomenon, which we call the cold war. What some of us may not realise is that the communist term for the cold war is 'peaceful co-existence'.

This apparent contradiction is hard for non-Marxists to swallow, but for Marxists there is no contradiction. For them, the cold war is what the British and Americans do when they try to counter communist subversion with anti-communist, or even non-communist ideas, for instance through the BBC or the Voice of America. When they talk about peaceful co-existence and ending the cold war, they mean freedom for communist parties everywhere to work for the overthrow of non-communist governments, while such governments refrain from taking counter-measures. Those who find this interpretation fanciful may care to read the two following excerpts from the World Communist Declaration of December 1960, to which eighty-one Communist parties, including those of the Soviet Union and China, subscribed:

> . . . By upholding the principle of peaceful co-existence, communists fight for the complete cessation of the cold war, disbandment of military blocs and dismantling of military bases, for general and complete disarmament under inter-national control, the settlement of international disputes through negotiation, respect for the equality of states and

their territorial integrity, independence and sovereignty, non-interference in each other's internal affairs, extensive development of trade, cultural and scientific ties between nations.

If words meant the same to communists as to non-communists, there would be nothing in this passage to which men of goodwill everywhere could possibly object. It is only human, after all, to long for peace and freedom from the fear of war. But words do not mean what they seem to mean when communists use them, for consider another passage from the same section of the World Communist Declaration:

> . . . Peaceful co-existence of countries with different social systems does not mean conciliation of the socialist and bourgeois ideologies. On the contrary, it means *intensification of the struggle* of the working class, of all the Communist parties, for the triumph of socialist ideas. But ideological and political disputes between states must not be settled through war. (My italics.)

There you have it, more or less in black and white: the cold war (i.e. anti-communist words and deeds) is to end, but communists everywhere are to intensify their struggle to overthrow non-communist governments, by all means short of war. Or rather, short of war between the great powers, for, as we shall see, some wars are held not to conflict with peaceful co-existence.

This brings me back to Mr Nan, whose words now take on a more precise meaning. For didn't he say it was the duty of Chinese communists to help 'the fighting Afro-Asian peoples'? Help them against whom? On this point, Mr Nan was only 50 per cent frank. Wielding statistics and balance sheets as weapons, he devoted the bulk of his speech to slaying imperialists, colonialists and neo-colonialists. These, he said, were the enemies who were keeping the fighting peoples of Afro-Asia in thralldom. What he refrained from saying—and this is hardly surprising if one remembers that he was speaking to Afro-Asians in Algiers—was that the African and Asian leaders

13

themselves were enemies, and would remain enemies until they allowed themselves to be led by the communists.

Does this interpretation also sound fanciful? Then consider the fact that the African and Asian leaders Mr Nan singled out for praise were the handful of men (such as Ben Bella of Algeria, Nasser of the UAR, Sukarno of Indonesia and Sihanouk of Cambodia) who had denounced western aid. By implication, those who do not denounce it are stooges of imperialism and neo-colonialism. At present, this means the vast majority of leaders of the under-developed countries.

In this context, what did that very senior personage of the Chinese leadership, Mr Chou En-lai, mean when he declared at the end of a seven-week tour of Africa early in 1964: 'Revolutionary prospects are excellent throughout Africa'? Revolution against whom? When Mr Chou spoke, most of the African countries had already achieved independence. He might, of course, have been referring to the Portuguese territories, which did not seem to be within sight of independence, but the context of his remarks made it plain that he was referring to all African countries that had not taken the revolutionary socialist path. Indeed the evidence is strong that in the last analysis, even such 'revolutionary' countries as Algeria, the UAR or Mali are regarded as proper targets for Peking's hostility, if not now then in the future, to the extent that their militant socialism deviates from Peking's model, for instance by too close an association with the Soviet Union.

The message, then is plain: Mr Chou was urging the violent overthrow of all African governments that maintain links with the western countries. Since these include even so militant a government as Algeria's (which, even under ex-President Ben Bella, was heavily dependent on French, and to a lesser degree on American, assistance) the sweeping nature of the Chinese Prime Minister's revolutionary call is clear. So, too, is the inner meaning of China's duty to help the fighting Afro-Asian peoples, as expounded by Mr Nan Han-chen.

* * *

In later chapters, I shall be giving factual examples of the kind of thing Chinese and other communists actually *do* in Africa, Asia and Latin America. But before that, we have to look at what they write and say. This is, of course, a tedious but inescapable aspect of communist studies. Although communist deeds and professions rarely match, the compulsion to demonstrate ideological purity remains strong in the communist world, even though it is no longer the monolithic entity it once was. Since real life diverges more and more from theory, ideology has, in fact, to be constantly revised.

So it has been, for instance, with the militant regimes of the Third World, to which Mr Nan referred in his Algiers speech. The emergence of these regimes has caused heart-searching and even anguish among communist theologists. According to the sacred writings of Marxism-Leninism, only revolutions led by Marxist-Leninists are acceptable. On the other hand, the appearance of militantly anti-western regimes, having reached power by revolutionary violence, was clearly an opportunity that could be turned to communist advantage. The ideological dilemma lay in the difficulty of establishing cooperative relations with such regimes while continuing to express reservations about their finality and the genuineness of their revolutionary credentials.

A few examples will show how agonising a dilemma it was. In Gamal Abdel Nasser's UAR, for instance, the Communist Party was illegal and its leaders were in gaol. The Algerian National Liberation Front (FLN) could not be expected to forget that in 1945, when an abortive uprising took place at Sétif, the French Communist Party was represented in General de Gaulle's post-liberation government, and that Algerian Communists took part with gusto in the bloody repression ordered by the French authorities. There was no Communist Party in the militantly anti-western nations of emerging Africa: Ghana, Guinea and Mali. In South-East Asia, even the powerful Indonesian Communist Party was kept out of the government until 1964 in President Sukarno's anti-western Republic. In

Latin America, the revolutionary Cuban regime was a problem in that Fidel Castro was no communist and had come to power without communist support (if one excepts the presence in his entourage of individual communists).

Cuba, on the other hand, was a particularly tempting morsel, conveniently close to the United States, increasingly dependent on communist economic aid, willing, perhaps, to be guided towards 'socialism' and well-placed to subvert continental America in the name of anti-*Yanqui* nationalism. There seemed a good chance that Cuba's revolution could be given a communist twist, but for this to happen it was necessary to find a way of making Cuba, and countries like Cuba, ideologically acceptable. The way was found at the conference of eighty-one Communist parties in Moscow in December 1960, which I have already mentioned. It was decided to launch a new designation for regimes like Cuba's, that might, with luck, be captured for communism. Henceforth these were to be known as 'independent States of national democracy'. To qualify for this title, a State would have to fight 'imperialism' (that is, the western countries), oppose (western) military bases on its soil, give full democratic rights to 'the people' (that is, the local Communist Party), and show its readiness to introduce 'democratic' (that is, socialist) reforms that would pave the way for communism.

It has become impossible to keep every member of eighty-one national delegations quiet, even if all are communists. So it soon became known that it was the Russians who had dreamt up the idea of 'national democracy', and that the Chinese had opposed it, only giving in for the sake of what turned out to be a short-lived unity of the world communist movement. There are indeed historical reasons for this divergence. By overthrowing the democratic Kerensky government in November 1917, Lenin had shown that a well-drilled Communist Party can gain control of somebody else's revolution.

Mao Tse-tung never liked this two-stage revolutionary

process. In his statement of 1940 on *New Democracy* he had postulated a dictatorship of several classes in alliance. And in July 1949, with victory in sight, he made it clear (in a further statement *On the People's Democratic Dictatorship*) that the Communist Party was to be firmly in control of its allies throughout the revolution.

It was not surprising, then, to find the Soviet press and Russian leaders, from Mr Khrushchev down, praising and explaining the concept of national democracy in the weeks and months after the World Communist Conference of 1960, while the Chinese kept quiet about it. This was a Russian idea, not a Chinese one.

Even the Russians, however, have often seemed puzzled by their own Machiavellianism. It is one thing to flatter anti-western regimes in the hope that they may accept Moscow's guidance on their future; but quite another when the same anti-western regimes insist on being anti-communist as well. Then on December 2, 1961—a year after the Moscow conference—Fidel Casto obligingly declared that he had been a Marxist all along (although he candidly explained that he had only read up to page 370 of Karl Marx's *Das Kapital* and didn't really understand Marxism when he had launched his revolution). This seemed to prove the Russians right after all. Fidel Castro was ready to usher in Stage Two of the revolution. He was being a Lenin to his own Kerensky, and there was no need to have him removed by communist revolutionaries, even if this had been politically practical.

One may doubt, however, whether the Russians have ever felt that their hold on this spellbinding but half-baked Marxist was secure. And how much more dubious must they feel about other revolutionary leaders who don't even claim to be Marxists?

Moreover, even the most anti-capitalist of the new regimes obstinately cling to non-Marxist ideas and even launch ideologies of their own—Burmese socialism, African socialism, Arab socialism and others that share the defect, in communist eyes,

17

of being the wrong kind of socialism. Of course the Soviet theorists hope that once a State has embarked on a 'non-capitalist' path of development it will in time turn to Marxism. But a nagging fear that this might not happen must lurk in their hearts.

Small wonder, then, that Soviet writers have veered this way and that when picking candidates for promotion to 'national democracy'. Guinea, the small West African State that stayed out of General de Gaulle's Community in 1958 and turned to the communist countries for help, looked a promising case. Then in December 1961, President Sékou Touré expelled the Soviet ambassador for meddling in Guinean affairs, and relations turned sour. General Ne Win's Burma was another likely candidate. But in November 1963 the General had hundreds of Burmese communists arrested, and Moscow was forced to think again.

Both Guinea and Burma, however, have been named as actual or potential States of national democracy. So has Bolivia, because of its 'democratic, anti-imperialist agrarian revolution' of 1952. So have Ghana and Mali, Algeria and the UAR. Before he fell, indeed, Mr Khrushchev took a deep plunge over the last two. In April and May 1964, President Ben Bella of Algeria (as he still was) was given the kind of reception Moscow usually reserves only for the great of the communist world. He stood beside Mr Khrushchev on the rostrum and was given the unprecedented honour—for a non-communist statesman—of being made a Hero of the Soviet Union. For good measure, Mr Khrushchev threw in an Order of Lenin and a Lenin Peace Prize. More significantly, perhaps, the final communiqué recorded an agreement that the Soviet Communist Party and the Algerian FLN should develop 'fraternal relations'.

Now this was a very revisionist thing for that ageing re-volutionary, Mr Khrushchev, to do. True, the 1960 World Communist Declaration had implicitly sanctioned aid to revolutionary regimes like Ben Bella's; but it drew the line at ideological endorsement of any regime that banned the local Communist Party, as Algeria's did. And in 1961 the Draft Programme of the Soviet Communist Party more explicitly rejected such heresy. Yet there was Mr Khrushchev approving fraternal relations between a Communist Party and a ruling party that had dissolved and absorbed its communist competitors.

On May 9, only three days after Ben Bella had left Moscow, Khrushchev was 'at it' again, this time in Egypt, where he had gone to inaugurate the first stage of the great dam at Aswan, built with Soviet help. President Nasser, too, became a Hero of the Soviet Union. But though Mr Khrushchev called his host 'comrade', and though Nasser had quietly freed a number of gaoled Egyptians in advance of the visit, there is evidence that on the ideological side, the two men didn't see eye to eye. On May 25, the semi-official paper *Al Gumhuriya* spoke of 'ideological friction between us and the USSR' during the Khrushchev visit.

Perhaps understandably, the guardians of doctrinal purity within the Soviet Communist Party did not take sympathetically to their master's fraternising with the ideologically impure revolutionaries of northern Africa. Khrushchev had his supporters of course, especially an outspoken propagandist called G. Mirski, who had paved the way for Khrushchev's plunge in articles describing Ben Bella and like-minded leaders as 'revolutionary democrats' and hinting that their regimes could skip rapidly into 'socialism' without the benefit of communist leadership. But other and more orthodox theoreticians, including that formidable and austere intellectual, Mikhael Suslov, were muttering and shaking their heads in disapproval. Another opponent was Boris Ponomarev, whose job was to keep up the Soviet Communist Party's links with brotherly parties that were not in power.

In the end, as we know, it was Suslov and his friends who got their way, and Khrushchev who was pushed out. From apparently deliberate leaks to the Italian communist press, much is known of the charges Mr Suslov made against his former boss. The one that interests us here is that Khrushchev had overstepped the mark in making Nasser a Hero of the Soviet Union without even consulting his colleagues beforehand.

Strangely, Khrushchev does not seem to have been taken to task for having made exactly the same award to Ben Bella. This may have been because the Algerian leader, although he had banned the Algerian Communist Party, had not gaoled its leaders, and indeed allowed prominent communists to air their views and even to give him advice.

True, these highly placed Marxists were not especially 'reliable' from Moscow's standpoint. One of them, for instance, was the Greek-born Michael Raptis, who had once been Secretary-General of the Trotskyist Fourth International. But even Raptis, though hardly a Moscow man, was always ready with anti-capitalist, anti-bourgeois and anti-western advice for the President, and therefore tactically a useful man to have around, from Moscow's viewpoint.

Ben Bella, however, dismissed his Marxist advisers early in 1965. Then, on June 19, he himself was overthrown in a military *coup d'état*, and the new revolutionary junta, headed by Colonel Boumedienne, soon made it clear that it would have no truck with communists. Mr Suslov and his friends must have thought how right they had been to doubt the wisdom of Khrushchev's comradeships.

* * *

The Chinese theorists never shared the doubts and anguish of Khrushchev and his friends or foes. In their eyes, everything was simple. There was only one truth: Mao's. And one orthodoxy: Peking's. The Russians, whether Khrushchev or his successors, are revisionists and therefore traitors. As for Ben Bella, Nasser and the rest, while they may deserve occasional pats on the back for anti-colonialism and anti-imperialism, they are not, of course, traitors. It is just that enlightenment has not yet reached them. It would never occur to the Chinese to treat such men, however tactically useful they might be, as honorary communists.

This is not surmise. Indeed it can be seen in black and white in the acrimonious public correspondence between the Soviet and Chinese Communist Parties. As we have seen, it was not the Chinese who thought up the 'national democracy' concept, but they seem to have accepted the original Russian idea of making use of anti-western revolutionary leaders while drawing the line at ideological acceptance of regimes that ban local Communist parties. When Khrushchev's friends suggested, in effect, that local communists could be sacrificed in the interests of anti-capitalist regimes, the scandalised Chinese replied (in a letter which *Pravda* published on July 14, 1963) that even if kings, princes and aristocrats were accepted as allies, local communists would still have to lead and control the revolution.

On certain tactical points, then, there was a divergence between Peking and Moscow. But the end result envisaged was the same, in that the emerging revolutionary leaders were to be used to facilitate the advent of communism. After all, even Khrushchev at his most revisionist and comradely never went as far as to say that Ben Bella and Nasser were communists. They could be called 'comrades'; but only because they looked like ushering in communism.

In fact, for all the venom with which Peking and Moscow attacked each other for ideological crimes, the theoretical differences between the two parties are a good deal narrower than many people may suppose. This is particularly true of their approaches to the so-called 'national liberation move-ment'. Here again, the master text is the World Communist Declaration of 1960—the last major communist statement to which both Moscow and Peking subscribed. Mr Nan Han-chen and his compatriots are not the only ones to feel a duty to-wards oppressed peoples. The communists of the eighty other parties who attended the 1960 meeting in Moscow also recognised

> . . . their duty to render the fullest moral and material assistance to the peoples fighting to free themselves from imperialist and colonial tyranny.

In other words, the communists felt they had a duty to help the national liberation movement. Once more, we are in the foggy realm of semantics. In the first instance, a national liberation movement is one that fights to free itself from colonial rule as, for instance, the Algerian FLN did. This is not all, however, for communists interpret 'imperialist and colonial tyranny' in a very special sense. It is not enough for a country to achieve independence, meaning sovereignty, for according to theory, imperialist exploitation persists *after* independence (when it is known as neo-colonialism). The process of national liberation, therefore, continues until all links with western countries have been severed and a country is firmly on the road to communism.

In this, the Russians and the Chinese are at one, as they are in the 'duty' they acknowledge to help national liberation movements. At this point I find it necessary to correct a widespread popular misapprehension. It is widely assumed that during the past few years the Russians have become peaceful while the Chinese, in contrast, are dangerous war-mongers. The truth is quite different. Certainly the Chinese are more bellicose than the Russians, at least verbally. But the Russians have by no means renounced war as an instrument of policy. True, they have come to the healthy conclusion that *nuclear* war is too costly to be practical (though nuclear war was just what Khrushchev risked when he installed rockets on Cuban soil in 1962). But they distinguish between accept-able and reprehensible wars, which they call 'just' and 'unjust' respectively.

A nuclear war is not acceptable because the Soviet Union might be destroyed. A 'local' war is defined as a war launched by 'imperialists' for their own ends, such as the Suez expedition of 1956. Local wars are doubly unjust: because they are imperialist and because they might escalate into a nuclear war. National liberation wars, however, are 'just' because they are anti-imperialist.

There is a dangerous inconsistency in this reasoning, in that a national liberation war (such as the war in South Vietnam) may well escalate into a local war, with built-in nuclear perils. But the communists, whether Russian or Chinese, choose to ignore such inconsistencies when it suits them. They don't oppose war as such, only wars that are not of their own choosing. Thus Khrushchev, in a speech on January 6, 1961, classified wars into the groups I have mentioned, and went on to say:

> There will be wars of liberation as long as imperialism exists, as long as colonialism exists. They are revolutionary wars. Such wars are not only permissible but inevitable. . . . What should our attitude be to such uprisings ? It should be most favourable.

On December 6, 1963, *Pravda* was even more specific when it declared that it was the Soviet Communist Party's duty to give all political and economic support to national liberation movements—*and if necessary, support by arms*. On May 11, 1964, speaking before the Egyptian National Assembly, Khrushchev took up the theme in a passage calling for the giving of weapons to nationalists struggling against imperialism. Now this is one issue on which Khrushchev's successors have not repudiated the deposed leader. On November 6, the new boss of the Soviet Communist Party, Mr Brezhnev, reaffirmed support, if necessary with arms, for the national liberation movement.

* * *

What does all this add up to ? It is not my purpose here to discuss the rights and wrongs of colonialism, imperialism and neo-colonialism, for I have already done so in previous books.

Here I am concerned with communist attitudes and behaviour towards the Third World. The behaviour will be dealt with later. As for the attitudes which have exercised our attention during the preceding pages, I think the evidence shows quite clearly that the communists, whether Russians or Chinese, are interested in liberation movements and anti-colonial struggles for communist purposes that may, for a while, happen to coincide with the ends of nationalist revolutionaries, but in the end are irrelevant to the needs of the emerging countries. In other words, they support these movements and these struggles for what they can get out of them.

It will be seen, in fact, that the Chinese have the following purposes in the Third World: to eliminate western and Soviet influence and to establish communism. The Russians, on their side, have these purposes: to eliminate western and Chinese influence and to establish communism. It will be seen that with one significant difference these aims are the same. But it would be quite wrong, as I hope to show, to conclude that the anti-Chinese efforts of the Russians and the anti-Soviet efforts of the Chinese simply cancel each other out. This conclusion is facile and therefore tempting. But it does not stand up to the evidence.

* * *

And now, perhaps, having started this chapter with a quotation from Mr Nan Han-chen's speech at an Afro-Asian economic seminar, I may end it by recording a small but significant incident in which he was the central figure.

Mr Nan wanted to read his speech in Chinese, which was not a conference language. He created a scene when the chairman ruled him out of order and was led, shouting protests, from the rostrum as an interpreter began to read his speech in French.

In itself, of course, this incident is of small moment, but it showed, not for the first time, that communism has by no means removed the ancient Chinese conviction of racial and cultural superiority. Indeed, far from removing or attenuating this conviction, communism seems to have heightened it, as the Russians, perhaps, know better than others; for throughout the long verbal exchanges marking the Sino-Soviet dispute, one factor has remained constant—Peking's insistence that reconciliation is possible only if the Russians acknowledge that the Chinese are right.

But what is true of China's attitude towards Russia is true also of its attitude to all the countries of the Third World.

2

The Rival Suns

IN 1953, when Stalin died, the monolithic empire of communism stretched from East Berlin to Shanghai. The giants of this empire, Russia and China, were united by a military alliance that seemed indissoluble. Whatever reservations Mao Tse-tung had about Stalin (whose advice he had ignored when conquering China), there was no doubt about who was Boss: in public, at any rate, Peking invariably deferred to Moscow.

But the Chinese have a saying that 'there cannot be two suns in the sky'. As early as 1949, Liu Shao-ch'i, now President of the Chinese People's Republic, had claimed that China's revolution was a model for the under-developed countries—the 'semi-colonial' countries, to use the communist catchphrase then in favour. Now in Moscow's eyes, there could only be one model—the Leninist or Soviet model. Liu's words must therefore have had an ominous ring of incipient challenge about them. And so it turned out: there could indeed only be one sun in the sky, and as the years went on, it became clear that in the eyes of the Chinese, Russia could not hope to be the sun in a world which, now as always, revolved around China, its eternal centre.

It is not part of my purpose to write a history of the Sino-Soviet dispute, for that has already been ably done by others (for instance, in a concise and accessible way, by Edward Crankshaw in his Penguin Special, *The New Cold War*). But a few things have to be said, at this stage, about a far-reaching quarrel that affects all of us, wherever we live, in more ways than we may care to think. The most important point, perhaps, is that it is not exclusively, or even primarily, about ideology, for as we have seen, the Soviet and Chinese positions on such important ideological issues as the 'national liberation movement' and war are closer than is often supposed.

This is not to say that there are *no* ideological differences between Peking and Moscow. Perhaps the most important ones, in the context of this book, concern the road to revolution. At the Twentieth Congress of the Soviet Communist Party, in 1956, Khrushchev had proclaimed that in some countries revolution might be achieved without violence, that is through parliamentary or otherwise constitutional means. This the Chinese fiercely repudiate: in their eyes, violent revolution will always be necessary. A deeper issue still is the 'model' which aspirant revolutionaries should turn to when they get down to business. I have already mentioned Liu Shao-ch'i's claim that the Chinese model is the only valid one for 'semi-colonial' territories. This, however, the Russians cannot and will not admit.

We glanced at the rival models in Chapter 1, but let us now look at them more closely. As we have seen, the Soviet theorists of revolution are content to let non-communists carry out a 'first-stage' revolution, as Kerensky's followers did in February 1917. The communists can then take over the revolution, in a second stage, by ousting the first-stage revolutionaries, as Lenin and the Bolsheviks did in November 1917. In contrast, Mao Tse-tung, Liu Shao-ch'i and the others insist that the communists—as the vanguard of the people—must remain in control throughout the revolution. That is one difference. Another is that the Soviet theorists allow local communists, should this be necessary, to maintain 'friendly' relations with the government in power, whereas Mao and Liu say they must be uncompromisingly hostile to the government, whether national or foreign. Mao's model is, in some respects, a more elaborate edifice than Lenin's. It was of course, based on China's own experience of 'protracted war' (which provided the title of one of Mao's books).

The Communist Party, said Mao, should form an arm of workers and peasants, to wage war against the government, described as the 'main enemy'. In time, 'liberated areas' will be won, and within these areas, the bourgeoisie and the 'middle peasants' (but not the 'rich peasants') can join the workers and poor peasants in a 'united front'. The liberated bases must be consolidated and enlarged, and the official armed forces harassed to the point of exhaustion, while the people's army is being built up. When the moment comes, the final offensive can be launched and 'national liberation' achieved. National liberation means simply the establishment of a so-called people's government under communist control. Once this has happened, the united front will have served its purpose—though its façade can be preserved—and the non-communist elements within it can be liquidated or made impotent.

This specifically Chinese theory was given a new gloss and a world-wide application in an article entitled 'Long Live the Victory of People's War', published throughout China on September 3, 1965. The author of this major policy-making statement was one of China's most famous soldiers, Marshal Lin Piao, Defence Minister and vice-chairman of the Politburo. In it, Lin called for the extension to the whole world of the Maoist theory of 'encirclement of the cities from the countryside'. On this world scale, he said, the capitalist countries were the 'cities', and Asia, Africa and Latin America were the 'countryside'. And he made it clear that the process of 'encirclement' could only be carried out by 'people's wars' led by communists who would take China's own revolutionary war as a model. Marshal Lin also made it clear that Russian communism had no part in this new China scheme of things.

In sum, these are not unimportant differences, but if the dispute were simply an ideological disputation, however acrimonious, it would be no more important, all proportions kept, than, say, a Cambridge Union debate, or if you prefer, a brawl about prices between the market women of Accra. But the real point of the 'ideological' split has always been over who gives the orders in the communist world. When Moscow and Peking simultaneously proclaim divergent doctrines, which of the two are the communists of the world supposed to obey? There is far more at stake, then, than the mere scoring of debating points.

Moreover, this is not simply a doctrinal quarrel, however important doctrine may be to communists: it is also, in a more fundamental sense, a clash between rival great powers—a clash that transcends ideology but is expressed in ideological terms because ideology provides the basis and justification of the Communist Party's monopoly of power in each of the rival giants. National as well doctrinal aims are at issue.

As a maturing industrial power, Russia could not be expected to have the same view of the world as a technically backward and largely under-developed country like China. The Soviet Communist Party wanted to preserve its monopoly of power, but the party leaders also wanted to preserve and extend the modest degree of economic affluence that had been achieved. In this context, they were becoming aware of an increasing divergence between doctrine and reality. Lenin, living in a world of limited destruction, could prophesy the 'inevitability' of war between the capitalist and communist states, leading of course to the liquidation of capitalism. But Khrushchev, living in the nuclear age, was aware that in a nuclear war there would be only losers. The Chinese communists, however, had no nuclear weapons and had less to lose, economically, than the Russians. Less to lose, and a far larger population—so that they could reckon on losing half their people and still emerging as one of the most populous nations on earth.

Thus it was that avoidance of nuclear war—that is, fundamentally, of war with the United States—came to be an important element in Khrushchev's foreign policy. Hence he proclaimed that war was now no longer 'fatally' inevitable. But this did not suit the Chinese at all. Mao wanted to keep his people under tension so that they would accept the sacrifices that were being imposed on them in the name of revolution. And for this purpose, it was useful, indeed essential, to preserve the image of America as the irreconcilable 'imperialist' enemy and hated stronghold of capitalism. It was on the issue of *nuclear* war, then, that Mao parted company with Khrushchev. It is unfair to the Chinese to say, as some people have said, that they actually advocate nuclear war; but it is true to say that they continue to consider war as inevitable, and maintain that it will destroy only capitalism, leaving communism victorious on earth.

Holding these views, Mao drew the militarily curious conclusion that Russia's possession of nuclear weapons had given the 'socialist camp' a decisive advantage over the 'imperialist camp'—so that while Khrushchev was working for a rapprochement with the United States, Mao was egging him on to bolder courses which Khrushchev considered 'adventurous'. Now that China has the beginnings of nuclear power it is quite possible that Peking will start to modify its views on nuclear war, though there was no sign of this when these lines were written. But in the years of worsening relations between Peking and Moscow, starting from 1956, not only did the Chinese not have nuclear weapons, but the Russians adamantly refused either to give them such weapons or to let them share the secrets of nuclear production. Later, as the dispute developed, the Chinese complained that the Russians had promised them weapons, but had let them down. This indeed was a major cause of friction between the two.

Another complaint, on China's part, was about Russia's policy of giving economic aid to non-communist countries of the Third World, especially Egypt and India, whereas the Chinese argued that any surpluses available should be reserved for China itself and other under-developed communist countries. Paradoxically, the Chinese themselves launched a rather selective aid programme of their own, but in this, as we shall see, they were competing with the Russians, as well as with the West. From 1959 on, when China's relations with India turned sour, an additional complaint was that the Russians, far from behaving like 'fraternal allies' of the

Chinese, were trying to be neutral between Peking and Delhi, and indeed supplying the Indians with arms. This again, was a national not a doctrinal issue. It served China's national interest, but not Russia's, to put the squeeze on India. The 'ideological' refinement of this situation was that Russia, in China's eyes, was in breach of the principle of socialist unity in failing to support Peking in its frontier dispute with India. It was this that made Khrushchev's behaviour so outrageous, from Mao's standpoint.

One can only guess at Russia's motives in staying out of the Sino-Indian dispute, and plausible ones are not hard to find. But one of the most plausible is probably the fact that the Russians were well aware that China had frontier claims against the Soviet Union, as well as against India. If Russia seemed to be supporting China's border claim against India, would this not strengthen China's hand in its latent claims against the territories of the Soviet Far East?

The fact of the matter is that Russia and China, despite their common anti-imperialist ideology, are themselves great imperial powers. The Soviet Union is the Tsarist empire, as restored by Lenin and expanded by Stalin. As for China, it has been plain, at least since 1949, that Mao Tse-tung, who is a great nationalist as well as communist leader, is intent on restoring the imperial greatness—and the imperial boundaries—of the Chinese empire at its height. This explains why Article 55 of the Common Programme adopted by the central committee of the Chinese Communist Party in September 1949, just before the proclamation of the People's Republic, laid down that the Republic would 'examine the treaties and agreements concluded between the Kuomintang (Chiang Kai-shek's Nationalist party) and foreign governments, and recognise, abrogate, revise or renegotiate them'. Since then, the Chinese have reconquered Tibet and concluded border agreements with Burma, Nepal, Pakistan, Afghanistan and Mongolia—but not with India or the Soviet Union. Yet on March 8, 1963, the Peking *People's Daily* listed four treaties imposed by Tsarist Russia on the decaying Chinese imperial government as among the 'unequal treaties' that would have to be revised.

* * *

In the deepest sense, then, the Sino-Soviet dispute is a great power clash, but the fact that it takes an ideological form is itself important. To non-communists, the ideological hair-splitting is tedious and irrelevant. If the Russians and Chinese want to quarrel over this or that point of doctrine, of what interest is it to outsiders? Why not sit back and let the disputants tear the world communist movement to pieces between them?

It is not difficult to sympathise with the viewpoint implicit in such rhetorical questions. But I do not share it. There are, in fact, dangers for all of us in the Sino-Soviet dispute, not least because the whole world—and above all the Third World—is the battleground for their rivalry. I don't mean to suggest that there is an imminent danger of war between the two communist great powers, though in the long run this danger cannot be ruled out in the light of what is known about border clashes along the Sino-Soviet frontier—the longest in the world. The dangers, it seems to me, arise from the com- mitment—common to Moscow and Peking—to support 'national liberation' movements in the Third World. The Chinese, as we shall see, are the pace-setters in the struggle to control these movements. Often the Russians seem to be dragging their feet, content with lip-service to national liberation. Then what might be called competitive subversion comes in. The Russians, in the last resort, cannot afford to let the Chinese communists gain a monopoly of influence among the guerrillas and revolutionaries. So whatever the Chinese do, the Russians must try to do as well.

Now this Soviet policy of support for 'national liberation' happens to be, by implication, in direct conflict with Russia's policy of nuclear peace and rapprochement with the United

States. Any wholehearted Russian support for guerrilla movements which the Americans oppose could lead, by escalation, to a direct clash between the Soviet Union and the United States. At this point, Russia's *State* policy is incompatible with Moscow's *party* policy.

China's policy is less contradictory than that. I happen to believe that the Chinese leaders live in a dangerous world of fantasy. The Russians have begun to perceive that the real world is not the same as the stereotype of Marxism-Leninism; and, ideology being the basis of State power, they are led into contradictions and embarrassments. The Chinese, in contrast, give no sign of having ever noticed that the real world is different from the dream world of Maoism. Unassailed by doubts, they achieve a continuing harmony of unreality between State and party. Worse, they try to impose their fantasies on others, as Mr Nan Han-chen did in Algiers.

For all these reasons, none of us, whatever our colour, or persuasion, wealth or poverty, can afford to remain indifferent to the Sino-Soviet struggle for the Third World.

3

With Gloves Off

THE Russians and Chinese seem to be as little concerned with the real interests of the Third World as Asians, Africans and Latin Americans are with the Sino-Soviet dispute. The African delegates who sprang to their feet at an Afro-Asian Solidarity conference in Algiers in April 1964 and told the communists how tedious it was when the Russians attacked Peking and the Chinese attacked Moscow, was speaking from the heart. Africans are not, of course, the only people who are bored by Sino-Soviet polemics. The boredom, however, must be overcome: after all, it is Africa's body that is being fought over. And not only Africa's, but Asia's and Latin America's bodies.

The energy and wordage expended by each side in attacking the other defies assessment and almost passes belief. To quote at length from the interminable speeches or articles emanating from the rival capitals of communism would make this book unreadable. What concerns us here is the truth of the proposition that the Russians and Chinese are hell-bent on excluding each other from the Third World. Certainly their words and deeds over the past two or three years have been consistent with this interpretation of their motives.

Since the Chinese have become the pace-setters in revolutionary communism, it will be useful to look first in their direction. In public, the Chinese are always careful to use arguments that will look properly Marxist-Leninist when exposed to dialectical scrutiny. The arguments they use in private are more interesting, for they violate what is supposed to be an inviolable Marxist-Leninist tenet in that they are frankly racialist. This is especially true of arguments intended for African ears. What the Chinese say, in effect, is they are

coloured people, like the Africans; and that they are therefore
particularly well qualified to champion the cause of oppressed
Africans; whereas the Russians are whites and fundamentally
the same as Americans or other whites in their attitudes
towards coloured people.

An early example of this was given at the Afro-Asian
Writers' conference in Cairo in 1962. On March 12, the
Kenya paper, *Daily Nation*, put it in these words:

> In private lobbying the Chinese are adopting an openly
> racist line. These Europeans, they say, are all the same
> whether they are French, Americans, Russians or Poles; we
> non-whites must get together. One Chinese delegate even
> went so far as to talk about the 'importance of us blacks
> sticking together'.

The same argument was used with increasing force by the
Chinese delegates to the Afro-Asian People's Solidarity conference at Moshi, in Tanganyika (as it then was) in February
1963. The Chinese mentioned the Cuban rocket crisis of the
previous October as proof that the Russians would 'let down'
the coloured peoples, and the 'agreement on co-existence
between Khrushchev and Kennedy' as a clear indication that
the Russians, as whites, were going to support the Americans.
Not long after, on August 8 that year, Mao Tse-tung entered
the arena with an impassioned declaration, calling for world-
wide support for the struggle of the American Negroes. The
Chinese leader's intention was not, one supposes, to align
himself with the civil rights programme of Presidents Kennedy
and Johnson. It was, in fact, simply part of the Chinese
campaign to identify China with the oppressed coloured
peoples.

Not unnaturally, the press in the Soviet Union and in the
countries that still, more or less, take their line from Moscow
have regarded the Chinese attempt to lump all whites together
as the 'most unkindest cut of all'. On November 5, 1963,
Pravda, the organ of the Soviet Communist Party, expressed
its pain indirectly through an article by Henry Winston,

chairman of the United States Communist Party, who declared that the coloured peoples on whose behalf Peking presumed to speak were aware that this was pure demagogy which 'smells of racialism from a long way off'. The Chinese, wrote Winston, were trying to deceive the peoples of Asia, Africa and Latin America. Similar views have been expressed in the newspapers of communist parties more or less faithful to Moscow, from Hungary to Mongolia.

The Chinese, on the other hand, are sensitive to charges that their racial arguments—which are never expressed in public—violate Marxist-Leninist principles. On October 31 and November 1, 1963, the Peking *People's Daily* carried extracts from anti-Chinese articles in the Soviet press. These were prefixed by an editorial note which complained of Soviet allegations that 'the Chinese statesmen have a slogan, "Down with the whites"', and commented:

> These remarkable anti-China articles are so badly written and the lies they tell are so ridiculous that they make repulsive reading.

The fact that African students have complained of racial discrimination in Peking, as well as in Moscow and east European capitals, is a sad comment on these strictures and recriminations.

* * *

In the Asian context, the racial content of Chinese arguments has been less in evidence. Instead, the Chinese have been insisting on the *imperialist* character of the Soviet Union. The most striking evidence of this emerged from the Afro-Asian Journalists' conference which met in Djakarta, from April 24 to 30, 1963. The conference launched an Afro-Asian Journalists' Association, as it was meant to, but the interesting thing is that the Soviet Union was excluded from this new body. This was a signal success for the Chinese. They did it through their Indonesian nominee for the chairmanship of the conference, Mr Djawoto of the Indonesia-China Friendship

Society, and other pro-Chinese delegates, some of whom were not even journalists.

So much is public knowledge. What is perhaps less widely known is that the Chinese delegates, in their private lobbying of other participants, argued that the Soviet Union should be kept out, on the ground that the Russians were imperialists who, like other European powers, were in Asia only by right of conquest. This argument implicitly rejected Lenin's contention that the status of non-Russian peoples and territories conquered in Tsarist times (and reconquered under Lenin's direction) had been altered by the emergence of 'people's power' in Russia in 1917.

There were racial subtleties to this ingenious argument, but these were implicit, not stated. By using the imperialist argument against Russia, the Chinese seemed to be leaving themselves wide open to the retort that the Chinese Han empire expanded into the Asian hinterland in much the same way as the Russian empire did, at the expense of non-Han peoples, such as Uighurs, Tibetans or Mongols. This is a perfectly valid counter-charge, but the Chinese knew what they were up to, and more importantly, whom they were speaking to. Unlike the Russians, the Chinese are Asians; and the Chinese knew that in their present mood, the leaders of the former western colonies in Asia—and elsewhere—are concerned only about *white imperialism*.

There was another and rather paradoxical point in China's favour. The Chinese People's Republic does not claim that its 'autonomous' regions, whose original populations were ethnically distinct from the Han Chinese, are independent. In contrast, the USSR's 'Union' republics, including the Asian republics of Tadzhikistan and Uzbekistan, are theoretically equal to the RSFSR (Russia proper). The fiction that these Soviet Asian republics are independent and equal members of the Soviet Union constitutes the main basis for the Soviet contention that the USSR is a non-imperialist Asian power. Since Tadzhik and Uzbek delegations are much in evidence in

38

Afro-Asian gatherings, this contention can be made to look convincing. It is, however, a fiction, and by exposing it, the Chinese were dealing a body-blow at Russian ambitions in the Third World.

★ ★ ★

In Latin America, where there is a considerable white population and independence from the former metropolitan powers—Spain and Portugal—is of long standing, the Chinese have tended to steer clear of racial and imperialist accusations against the Russians. Instead, they have sought to exploit the supposed attractions of the young and revolutionary Chinese Communist Party for the youth of Latin America, a tactic that makes sense in the light of the high proportion of under-40s in the population.

In addition to the usual accusation that the Soviet Communist Party is no longer Marxist-Leninist, the Chinese use the argument that the men who run the Soviet Union have grown too fond of the material benefits associated with an affluent society, to which they aspire without having quite achieved it. The youth of the Soviet Union, say the Chinese, has lost its revolutionary fervour and is therefore unable to provide appropriate leadership for young Latin Americans within such communist 'front' organisations as the World Federation of Democratic Youth and the International Union of Students.

As in the case of the racial argument, this one has been echoed in Soviet and Chinese information media. Thus on August 17, 1963, Moscow Radio, describing the activities of Chinese 'fraternal delegates' at a student seminar in Bahia, Brazil, in July, accused the Chinese of slandering Soviet youth. The Chinese, Moscow radio added, had been trying to keep the USSR out of a conference of Latin American, Asian and African students which Peking had been advocating. Earlier (on July 19 and 20), the official New China News Agency had claimed majority support for China from Brazilian students.

Another line of argument used by the Chinese in Latin America is that their model for revolution is especially suited to the largely peasant societies of that vast area. They have also played on the supposed ethnic similarities between themselves and the American Indians, particularly in Peru and other Andean countries where the backwardness and poverty of Indian populations whose forefathers built great empires constitute, at least in theory, a fertile soil for subversive propaganda.

In this context, Cuba must be seen in Peking as at once an opportunity and a source of frustration. An opportunity, because Fidel Castro's was a peasant revolution, albeit led by bourgeois intellectuals. But a frustration, too, because Cuba is heavily dependent on Soviet help which China is unable to match, even though Cuba's guerrilla war specialists are doing just what China itself would like to do in Latin America in fomenting uprisings among the peasants. Indeed in a doctrinal sense, the Cuban revolution is a curious hybrid, neither fish nor fowl. The Russians point to the Cuban experiment as an example of Lenin's two-stage revolution, since it was not communist at the outset, but came under communist control later. The Chinese, however, can also claim paternal affinities, in that the Cuban revolutionaries ousted the dictator Batista through guerrilla warfare, the setting up of liberated areas and a final offensive (in Cuba's case, a walkover, but this doesn't affect the point) against the forces of the established government.

* * *

I have already mentioned the wrangling that goes on between the Russians and Chinese within the Afro-Asian movement. Let me now place the story in its context and carry it further. I have used the term 'Afro-Asian movement' for convenience, but it calls for definition. To most people it suggests the important but diffuse current of opinion that led to and grew out of the first great Afro-Asian conference, held at Bandung in 1955. At that time, the Asian ex-colonies were independent, but the African ones were not. A kind of unity, albeit imperfect, emerged from the remembered colonial slights of the Asians and the continuing struggle of the Africans. That was one important thing about Bandung. Another was that China was represented, as an unquestionably Asian power, while the Soviet Union, despite its vast Asian territories, was not.

This was a blow to Soviet dreams of identification with the anti-colonial movement in the Third World, and the Russians set about creating an Afro-Asian bandwaggon of their own, on to which they might jump. Their technique was to set up Asian Solidarity committees in various countries, with the help of local Communist parties. In time, these were renamed *Afro-Asian* Solidarity committees, and in 1957 an Indian Communist persuaded President Nasser of Egypt to convene an Afro-Asian Solidarity conference in Cairo. Out of this emerged a permanent Afro-Asian Solidarity office in Cairo, with a Secretariat on which the Soviet Union and China were re-presented—under an Egyptian secretary-general. The Russians had thus got in by the back door of Cairo, having failed to gain admission by the front door of Bandung.

In 1957, the Chinese were still ready to accept Soviet leader-ship of the world communist movement, whatever their private reservations. And if the Russians wanted to be regarded as honorary Afro-Asians, the Chinese were not, at that stage, prepared to blackball their admission to the Solidarity club. As the Sino-Soviet dispute developed, however, they began to have second thoughts until, as we have seen, they started spreading racialist and imperialist accusations against the Russians and actually had them excluded from the Afro-Asian Journalists' Association.

This was treachery enough, from Moscow's point of view, but it soon became clear that it was only the beginning of a campaign to get Russia drummed out of the Afro-Asian move-ment altogether. The Journalists' Association was to be the forerunner of a number of other Afro-Asian organisations, to be formed without Russian membership, and in which Chinese influence was to be paramount. Students, scientists and trade unionists were to be roped in, to form new front organisations in rivalry to the Soviet-controlled World Federation of Democratic Youth, the World Federation of Trade Unions and many similar organisations set up by Stalin's order in Prague and elsewhere after the Second World War.

The climax to all this was to be the 'second Bandung', from which, if the Chinese had their way, the Russians would have been excluded. The conference was to be held in Algiers at the end of June 1965, and as the date drew near, Peking's attacks on the Russian 'revisionists', whether in public or in private, grew ever shriller. To some 'Afro-Asians', notably the Algerians, who were to be the hosts of the conference and who, at that time, were still on close terms with the Russians, Peking's behaviour was highly embarrassing. In the end, however, the issue of whether or not Russia was to be invited was unceremoniously resolved by the military coup d'état that unseated President Ben Bella on June 19, a few days before the conference was due to open.

The coup spared the Russians the possible humiliation of a snub from the Afro-Asian world; but neither Moscow nor Peking could derive comfort from it. The Chinese immediately recognised the new Algerian regime, but gained nothing from it, as the conference was postponed. The Russians held their hand—and their breath—but soon found that the new Algerian leader, Colonel Boumedienne, was hostile towards Soviet influence in his country. While the Soviet press remained silent, all the pro-Russian communist newspapers in western Europe (and in Cuba) lashed out at the new regime as 'anti-revolutionary'. The Chinese, on their side, piously declared that they did not interfere in other people's affairs. Some African and Asian leaders, who knew better, may have smiled wrily as they listened.

In the end, the whole issue of a 'second Bandung' petered

out in a fiasco in which the Chinese were the main losers. A new date had been set for the conference—November 5. But on October 28, Peking abruptly announced that China would boycott it. By that time, it looked as though the Russians were going to be there. The Egyptians had blessed their presence, and the Chinese may have got wind of the fact that the Algerians, too, favoured Russian attendance, as indeed they said they did three days after Peking's boycott announcement. But in a negative sense, the Chinese did get their way, since the conference was called off altogether.

II

The New
Scramble for Africa

I

Competitive Approaches

IT WAS President Nyerere of Tanzania who said it. What was happening, he told the Third Afro-Asian Solidarity Conference at Moshi in Tanganyika in February 1963, was 'the second scramble for Africa'. And he made it clear that he was referring not only to the struggle between East and West but also to that between the Russians and the Chinese.

Dr Banda echoed him. Dr Hastings Banda, President of Malawi (formerly Nyasaland), is a true and militant African nationalist if ever there was one. He is also a realist, well aware, in particular, of the realities of Africa and what is going on there. On September 11, 1964, Dr Banda called a press conference at Zomba. The subject, he said, was communist China, and he added:

> We are having a second scramble for Africa—not so much for the body of Africa as for its soul. . . . Although their own people have not enough to eat, they find enough money to corrupt African politicians everywhere. Only politicians of honesty and character can stand up to them.

A few days earlier, Malawi's President had dismissed several of his ministers who, he told the National Assembly, on September 8, would have murdered him in cold blood. But the real culprit at the end of Dr Banda's accusing finger was the Chinese ambassador in Dar-es-Salaam. It was under the ambassador's 'steering hand', said Dr Banda, that the dismissed ministers had tried to stir the people up against him. Moreover, he went on, the Chinese ambassador had told one of the ministers that Malawi would receive a loan of £18 million if it granted recognition to the Chinese communist government.

47

Next day, an official of the Chinese embassy in Dar-es-Salaam described Dr Banda's allegations as 'a fantastic fabrication and complete nonsense'. Dr Banda, however, knew what he was talking about. The Chinese have been extraordinarily free with their rather meagre supply of foreign currency in Africa. I am not referring simply to loans to African States (some of which may fulfil legitimate purposes), but to such things as bribes to politicians, 'scholarships' and travelling money for Africans who are taken to Peking to learn terrorist techniques, and similar undercover uses of money. A number of Congolese rebels, for instance, have received Chinese money; quite large sums are known to have reached, among others, Mr Oginga Odinga, the Vice-President of Kenya, who indeed has made no secret of it.

Nor am I suggesting that the African politicians who take Chinese (or Russian) bribes are necessarily selling their souls. Nationalists and politicians are often in need of funds, and the tradition of acceptance is fairly well established in Africa. Gratitude and subservience may follow; or may not. The Chinese can never be sure they have actually bought what they paid for. What is interesting is that they should be *trying* to buy African souls.

What Dr Banda said about a second scramble for Africa is also true, and indeed is simply a picturesque way of describing what is actually happening before the eyes of all Africans. With some exceptions, the withdrawal of European power has been quicker, and the new administrations have been more rudimentary, in Africa than in Asia. The power vacuum has been correspondingly greater, and the communists have moved in—scrambled in if you prefer—to fill the gap.

The direct interest which the communist powers now take in Africa is relatively recent. In the old colonial days, when the world communist movement was a monolithic monster jumping to the crack of Moscow's whip, the Soviet Union was content to leave subversion in the colonial territories to the communist parties of the metropolitan powers. If the Russians wanted to stir up trouble in, say, the Belgian Congo or Ghana, they would give the appropriate orders to the Belgian or British Communist Party, which would then take the required action. An exception to this rule seems to have been South Africa, which had a Communist Party of its own—one of the earliest of its kind, established by the Comintern (through which Moscow controlled communists everywhere) in 1921.

After the Second World War, the Russians concentrated their attention on East Asia, where the British, French and Dutch colonies were achieving or fighting for independence. For various reasons, it was more difficult, as well as less timely, to put a comparable effort into undermining Africa. For one thing, most of the continent was still under colonial rule, and most of the local communist parties or groups had been banned at some stage or other (the South African Communist Party was dissolved by decree in 1950) and it was difficult to set up clandestine bodies under the noses of the European-run security services or special branches. For another thing, the communist theorists hadn't clearly thought out how to go about the job of subversion in the special circumstances of Africa.

The self-imposed duty of communists to undermine and overthrow the colonial order was not, however, entirely neglected. Lacking secure or reliable Communist parties in Africa, the Russians and their communist friends in western Europe worked through various front organisations, above all through the World Federation of Trade Unions (WFTU). This was particularly useful in French-speaking Africa, for many African leaders (including, for instance, Sékou Touré, later President of Guinea) were members of the French Confédération Générale du Travail (CGT) itself affiliated to the WFTU.

The first signs of a real Soviet attempt to study Africa and interpret it according to Marxism-Leninism came in 1954, with the publication in Moscow of a symposium called *The Peoples of Africa*. Understandably, since the Russians had virtually no first-hand knowledge of Africa, this work was compiled mainly from foreign sources. In March 1957, the month of Ghana's independence, Moscow radio announced the forthcoming publication of fifty-five books on 'the struggle of the peoples of Africa against colonialism and for their rights'. Moscow's studies were clearly making progress.

It was about this time that foreign students of Soviet communism first began to hear the name of Ivan Izosimovich Potekhin. During the next seven years, until his death in 1964, aged 61, it was hardly possible to bracket the Soviet Union and Africa without throwing in Professor Potekhin's name for proper measure.

The late Professor was certainly Russia's leading Africanist, but his academic distinction alone might not have accounted for the prestige and high positions that came his way during his last ten years of life. At least as important to his career was the fact that he was a loyal and tested communist. When he entered the Leningrad Institute of Oriental Studies in 1930, he had already been a member of the Communist Party for ten years. His special study was the peoples and problems of Africa, with particular reference to Swahili and the Bantu people of South Africa. Two years later, he was organising a department of African studies at the Institute, and in 1955, he took a degree of 'Doctor of historical sciences'. His thesis was entitled 'The Formation of a National Society among the Bantu'. Note the title, for it provides a clue to what Potekhin was trying to do, which was to interpret Africa in Marxist terms.

This was not easy. African society, with its tribal sub-divisions and communal traditions, didn't easily lend itself to Marxist analysis. There didn't seem to be 'classes' as Marx understood the term. The working class, in particular, was in its infancy. To a communist, however, Marx can never be wrong; nor can there be exceptions to the 'laws' of social development, leading inevitably to class struggle, revolution and the establishment of communism. The whole purpose of

Potekhin's studies, from 1932 on, was to fit Africa into the pattern of Marxist analysis. An unkinder way of putting it was that he was trying to twist the facts of Africa to fit communist theory.

Professor Potekhin published some of his findings in a much quoted article in *Kommunist*, the theoretical organ of the Soviet Communist Party. This was in June 1957. There is little point in requoting this article here, however, for it was superseded, in effect, by a booklet published in Moscow in 1960—Africa's year—and entitled *Africa Looks to the Future*, which may be said to have embodied Potekhin's definitive views on Africa and Marxism. The conclusions Potekhin reached in this booklet *are* worth recalling for they show how much more deeply Potekhin was interested in Marxism and its acceptance by Africans, than in the interests of the Africans themselves.

Africa, said Potekhin, had 'a vocation for socialism'. The trouble was that Africans didn't seem to know true socialism from false. He quoted a number of differing African definitions of socialism, by leaders like Presidents Senghor (Senegal), Nyerere (Tanganyika), Nkrumah (Ghana) and Nasser (UAR), and by the Senegalese intellectual Jacques Janvier, who wanted Africans to take Yugoslavia as a model. One by one, Potekhin chided these distinguished Africans: there was only one kind of socialism for Africa, he said—the Marxist variety.

The advocates of 'African socialism' were on the wrong track, said Potekhin, because they wanted to build socialism on the peasantry. It was true, he conceded, that 'class formation' was still incomplete in Africa, but already millions of Africans worked for hire. These constituted a proletariat and were being organised into trade unions. Africa, he said firmly, could not be an exception to Marxist-Leninist theory.

Potekhin wrote his booklet at the time when the communist theory of 'neo-colonialism' was beginning to catch on among non-communist leaders in Africa and elsewhere in the Third World. So it was not surprising to find him arguing that the advent of independence did not complete the process of decolonisation. The last vestiges of colonialism must be removed, he insisted. This meant that independent economies must be established, with communist economic assistance. Each emerging State must have its own national currency. Imperialist, political and military bases must be removed. Artificial linguistic divisions, too, must go (this was a reference to the difficulties of communication between French-speaking and English-speaking Africans). As a corollary, the national languages of the Africans must be re-established.

Having reported Potekhin's views, I shall allow myself a comment or two. What he wrote about African socialism speaks for itself; and I have said all I need say about neo-colonialism in the Background Book of that name. But it is worth pointing out that at the time Potekhin's book appeared, the only emerging African country with an independent national currency was Guinea and that Guinea's bank notes, printed in Czechoslovakia, were worthless on the international money market. Independence doesn't necessarily bring prosperity.

Potekhin's linguistic recommendation was perhaps more worrying still. It was true enough that French-speaking Africans have to learn English to understand their English-speaking cousins. But if Africans followed Potekhin's advice, cutting out the 'imperialist' languages and reverting to a multitude of tribal tongues, the great majority of which still have no written form, they would be substituting a Babel of barriers for the present relatively simple one of French-English (and Italian if one includes Somalia). Not only would African State be cut off from African State, but even African tribal units within each State would be isolated; and outraged as well, probably, for no one supposes that, say, Luo-speaking Kenyans would like it if Kikuyu became the national language of Kenya.

Moreover, the re-establishment of 'national' languages would deny studious Africans access to the world of knowledge and communication available through mastery of one of the world's great languages. (Perhaps, however, Potekhin really meant to suggest that Africans should start learning Russian instead of French and English.) There is no denying that many African nationalists would be happy if their ancestral tongues could become official languages. But they are not unaware of the practical drawbacks and, in general, see Potekhin's recommendations for the nonsense they are.

From a Marxist standpoint, however, Potekhin's arguments made sense, since their concern was not with Africa's needs but with their receptiveness to Marxist persuasions.

* * *

The Chinese seem to have done far less theorising about Africa than the Russians, and to have been even more opportunistic in exploiting situations not foreseen by the textbooks. I have already described the Maoist theory of revolution in some detail. In one sense, Africa conformed to Mao's theory, but not in another. Like China, Africa is a mainly peasant society; unlike those of China, Africa's communists are few, weak and disunited. Faced with this situation, the Chinese, as we shall see, have concentrated their subversive efforts on *any* group that seemed potentially able to cause a breakdown in law and order, quite regardless of its political complexion. One of the most striking examples of this opportunism concerns the neighbouring central African States of Rwanda and Burundi— formerly the Belgian colony of Ruanda-Urundi, which we shall examine in detail in a later chapter. For the moment, since we are concerned with theory at this point, let me simply quote from a Chinese army document, dated 1961, which gives a fair idea of the way the Chinese think about Africa:

> Some places in Africa are like our country at the time of the Boxer Rebellion, some are at the stage of the 1911 Revolution, some are at the period of the May 4 movement. None have reached the period of the Northern Expedition, or the period

of the anti-Japanese resistance, and they are far from the 1949 era of China. What matters now in Africa is anti-imperialism and anti-colonialism; anti-feudalism is not yet important. It is time, not for social revolution, but for national revolution, time for a broad united front. In Africa there are many Rightists, not many Leftists in power and the number of those in the centre is not large. The Rightists must lose their prestige and position; then other people should come forward who will carry out the national revolution.

If there were one or two among the independent countries which would effect a real nationalist revolution . . . a revolutionary wave would roll up the African continent.

One needs, perhaps, to remember that when these words were written, a number of African countries were already independent, and it is quite clear from the second paragraph I have quoted that the Chinese were hoping their governments would be overthrown by 'real' nationalists and revolutionaries. Is this, one wonders, what Nasser and Banda, Nkrumah and Kenyatta fought for? One wonders, too, how many African leaders had read the document from which I have quoted when Chou En-lai told a mass rally in Mogadishu, Somalia's capital, that 'revolutionary prospects are excellent throughout the Africa (the phrase already quoted on page 14).

This was Mr Chou's parting shot after a seven-week tour of Africa in 1964. But he came back to the charge during his second African tour, when, at a rally in Dar-es-Salaam on June 5, 1965, he declared: 'An exceedingly favourable situation for revolutions prevails today not only in Africa, but also in Asia and Latin America.'

This time, Chou's inflammatory words did not go un-challenged. Speaking in Chou's presence, his host, President Nyerere, said that 'at no time shall we lower our guard against the subversion of our government or our people'. True, these were guarded words, and they occurred in a speech in which President Nyerere also attacked 'neo-colonialism'. But in neighbouring Kenya, the government took the rare step of issuing a statement commenting on Chou's revolutionary declaration of June 5. 'It is not clear to the Kenya government', the statement ran, 'what type or form of revolution he has in mind. But the Kenya government intends to avert all revolutions, irrespective of their origins or whether they come from inside or are influenced from outside.'

This was clear enough. And it was perhaps not surprising that the invitations Chou En-lai had hoped to get from various African countries did not materialise and that he found himself flying back to Peking only eight days after touching African soil. Revolution, it seemed, was less popular than he had supposed.

2

The Yellow Hand

---

*Burundi is the way to the Congo, and when the
Congo falls the whole of Africa will follow.*
—Mao Tse-tung

IN MAY 1964, Tung Chi-ping, a young interpreter, walked
out of the Chinese embassy in Bujumbura and sought asylum
with the Americans. Some months later, the Department of
State in Washington released part of the text of a statement he
had made. It was he who quoted the saying at the head of this
chapter, which he attributed to Mao Tse-tung. Whether or not
the ageing sage of Chinese communism used these words, it
does seem that the quotation was in constant use among the
staff of the Chinese embassy in the euphonious capital of the
Kingdom of Burundi. Until, that is, January 29, 1965, when
Burundi suspended diplomatic relations with the Chinese
People's Republic, threw a cordon of military police around
the embassy and expelled the staff, down to the last phoney
'domestic servant'.

The number of servants had, in fact, shot up surprisingly
after a Burundi order in October 1964, which laid down that
no more than eight nationals of any country should be accredited as diplomats in that country's embassy. By that time there
were about twenty Chinese 'diplomats' in this small capital of
a central African State, remote from the Middle Kingdom to
which Mao Tse-tung was heir. The embassy claimed it had
complied with the order, but it was noticed that just as many
Chinese seemed to be working at the embassy as before.
Twelve of the 'diplomats', however, had become 'domestic
staff'. It was all a question of definition.

What were the Chinese communists doing with an embassy of this size in a remote country where China's formal

commitments were almost non-existent? Indeed while the build-up of staff was going on, there weren't even any aid or cultural agreements to be administered, although a trade agreement had been signed in October 1964 (rumours that the Chinese wanted to establish commercial and cultural missions in addition to their already swollen embassy staff may have had something to do with Burundi's alarm at the diplomatic invasion from Peking). Nor was there a large Chinese community in Burundi, such as might have justified a numerous consular staff.

The Chinese communists, did, however, 'need' a large staff in Burundi—not for normal diplomatic work but for three undercover aims that became apparent to Burundi itself as time went on: to train, arm and finance rebels from the neighbouring Congo; to give similar help to rebels in Rwanda; and to undermine Burundi itself.

Diplomatic relations between Burundi and China were established in December 1963. A man who must have been particularly pleased with himself when this happened was a 'journalist' called Kao Liang. Ostensibly Kao Liang was the New China News Agency's correspondent in East Africa. In reality, he was a trouble-shooter for the Chinese Foreign Ministry. Well-known in Kenya, Tanganyika and elsewhere, he had been particularly active in Burundi, generous with gifts to Burundians in high places and persuasive in his talk of China's mission to help the peoples of Africa. What he didn't say was that it was a matter of indifference to Peking whether aid went to one African people or another, so long as the outcome was unrest. Nor did he make it clear that much of the aid would be designed to help African peoples fight each other.

Behind the high palisade of the Chinese embassy, strange things seemed to be going on. There were regular cinema shows, at which Mao Tse-tung's techniques of guerrilla warfare were explained on celluloid. Arms and cash were distributed and lectures were given. The arms had been landed, it is thought, in Dar-es-Salaam on Tanganyika's coast, then sent by rail and road to Bujumbura. The money was lavish. Congolese rebels were offered a year's pay in advance by the generous Chinese, who also helped with military training in rebel camps in Burundi.

Strategically, this made sense, as a glance at a map of central Africa will show. Mao, or the men who spoke in his name, had spotted the obvious fact that rebels in Kivu province in the eastern Congo could be fed and supplied from Burundi.

But if the establishment in Burundi of a training base for Congolese rebels made strategic sense, the whole exercise was ideologically puzzling. Why were the Chinese so eager to make their mark in the 'feudal' monarchy of Burundi, home of the long and lordly Tutsi, those imperialists of central Africa, instead of the people they had so long oppressed in neighbouring Rwanda? Indeed the 'slave people' of Rwanda, the Hutu, had risen against the Tutsis in 1959, driven them out and set up a peasant republic of a kind that Mao might have been expected to encourage. But the Hutu lacked one thing which the Tutsis of Burundi had: the right place on the map—right, that is, as a stepping stone to Stanleyville. It was the Tutsis, therefore, who were to be cajoled and supported.

China is not, of course, the only power in history to be guilty of ideological opportunism. But the tragic circumstances of the Tutsi-Hutu blood feud made Chinese behaviour harder to stomach than it might have been. More than 150,000 Tutsis had fled to Burundi, Uganda, Tanganyika and the Congo during the Hutu uprising. Among them was the former Mwami, or King, of Rwanda, Kigeri V, who soon began organising his followers into a kind of army. The Tutsi raids on Rwanda territory roused the Hutu to genocidal fury. Within weeks, tens of thousands of Tutsis still living in Rwanda were hacked to death; neither women nor children nor the old and sick were spared.

There is perhaps little that can be done by the outside world in a crisis of atavistic vengeance. But Tanganyika had offered land on which the giant former overlords could be resettled, and the International Red Cross had worked out how to take them there, house them and start them on their new life. The Chinese communists, however, chose to pour more fuel on the fire—by giving arms and money to the ex-Mwami, by training and arming his Tutsi followers, by importing professional agitators from China and by shipping at least one group of Tutsis to China for training in terrorism, sabotage and guerrilla warfare.

For such extra-diplomatic work, the Chinese embassy in Bujumbura did indeed need a larger staff than the purely diplomatic routine would have required. But there was more. The Chinese diplomats moved energetically among Burundians, inviting this man to China, bribing that man with money or gifts.

Until the autumn of 1964, this lavishness and persistence had yielded dividends. Mr Albin Nyamoya, who had become Prime Minister in April that year, had shown himself singularly receptive to Chinese suasions. The Mwami of Burundi, Mwambutsa IV, decided, however, that enough was enough. He removed Nyamoya and on January 11, 1965, reappointed a former Prime Minister, Mr Pierre Ngendandumwe, in his place. It was a short-lived Premiership, for four days later, Ngendandumwe was shot in the back as he was leaving the maternity hospital where his wife had just given birth to a son.

I know of no clear evidence of Chinese complicity in this assassination. But the inquiry that followed uncovered large stocks of Chinese ammunition. This was too much for the Burundians, and the Chinese were sent home.*

* * *

The story of the Chinese embassy in Bjumbura is closely paralleled by that of the embassy in Congo-Brazzaville. There

* The first concern of new military regimes that seized power in Dahomey, Upper Volta and the Central African Republic between November 25, 1965 and January 5, 1966, was likewise to get rid of 'their' Chinese diplomats.

again, a glance at the map will show why. If Bujumbura looked like China's road to Stanleyville, Brazzaville was even more obviously a stepping stone to Leopoldville: the two cities— one in the former French Congo and the other in the former Belgian Congo, face each other across the broad and powerful Congo river. This might not have mattered if two things hadn't happened: in August 1963, the right-wing ruler of Congo-Brazzaville, the Abbé Fulbert Youlou, was overthrown by the 'progressive' followers of M. Massemba-Débat; and in October, a group of Congolese dissidents, having failed in an attempted *coup d'état*, fled across the river to Brazzaville.

In combination, these circumstances spelled opportunity for the watchful Chinese. In February 1964, they set up shop in Brazzaville, opening an embassy that soon grew, as the Bujumbura embassy was growing, to twenty very active 'diplomats'. Loans, technical assistance and flattery were forthcoming for M. Massemba-Débat's administration and it was, perhaps, fitting that he himself should have gone to Peking for the fifteenth anniversary celebrations of the Chinese People's Republic on October 1, 1964.

More interesting, however, was what the Chinese were up to behind the scenes. The Congolese rebels had set up a Conseil National de Libération and launched an armed rebellion against the Congolese central government in Kwilu province. One of the rebel leaders was Pierre Mulele, a former Minister of Education in the government of the late and murdered Patrice Lumumba. Now Mulele is reported to have spent two years in China, undergoing a graduate course in subversion and guerrilla techniques. According to one report, some 200 of Mulele's followers were given tickets to China, for study at the Chinese War Academy.

By definition, such reports are hard to check, but there is nothing inherently improbable in them. It is known, for instance, that the swollen staff of the Chinese embassy at Brazzaville includes two military advisers who have been helping to train Congolese rebels in camps at two places:

Gamboma and Impando. The Counsellor at the embassy, Colonel Kan Mai, a former military attaché at Katmandu in Nepal, was thought, in the autumn of 1964, to be the 'driving force' behind the rebels. It is known, moreover, that the embassy provided the Conseil National de Libération with money and a particularly useful gift in kind—a 75-kilowatt radio transmitter. Captured Chinese arms and 'Maoist' instruction manuals have also served to give the game away.

* * *

China's intervention in Africa was indeed already of long standing before the Congolese rebellions broke out. The Peking *People's Daily* was able to claim, as early as December 1961, that Chinese pamphlets on guerrilla warfare were circulating widely in Africa. A year earlier, six Africans were arrested in the Cameroons, on their return from China. They and three others had completed a ten-week course at a military academy just outside Peking. They had been taught how to make explosives, grenades and mines, and trained in the use of more elaborate weapons. The demolition of telephone installations, bridges and railways was on the curriculum; and so, it need hardly be said, was political indoctrination.

The six men had their orders. They were to make contact with the ALNK, standing for the National Liberation Army of Kamerun (spelt with a 'k', German-style), the terrorist left wing of the UPC or Union of the Peoples of Cameroun (confusingly spelt with a 'c', French-style).

A point to note is that the French Cameroun became independent in January 1960. But this stopped neither the subversive terrorism of the ANLK nor Peking's active support of it. In Peking's eyes as in Moscow's, a country becomes independent only when it has entrusted its destinies to Marxist-Leninists; and the left wing of the UPC conformed to this definition. Here as elsewhere, opportunism remains the password to China's African policy; for in September 1964, a Chinese trade and goodwill mission turned up in Cameroun, where President Ahidjo was still in power despite Chinese efforts to unseat him and extend the massacres of the ANLK.

In their search for trouble-making opportunities, the Chinese have naturally devoted much attention to that bubbling centre of revolutionary activity, Dar-es-Salaam, capital of Tanzania (as Tanganyika and Zanzibar have been jointly known since April 1964). It is there that the 'Liberation Committee' of the Organisation of African Unity has its headquarters. Tanganyika was the first East African State to achieve independence, and it was perhaps natural that Dar should become a place of refuge for the 'Freedom Fighters' of southern, central and eastern Africa. And not merely of refuge but of training in the techniques of insurrection. It is not surprising, then, that the large Chinese embassy at Dar has been generous with funds and offers of training facilities for Freedom Fighters. It is probably true, indeed, to say that the Dar embassy is Peking's main springboard for action in Africa.

Wherever there are training centres for guerrilla fighters or bomb-throwers, however, you will find Chinese communist traces. Tlemcen, in Algeria, is another case in point. Ex-President Ben Bella of Algeria regarded Tlemcen as his very militant regime's top revolutionary showpiece. For seven years, the Algerian Front de Libération Nationale fought the French for independence. Now Algeria has more arms and specialists in guerrilla fighting than it can use within its own borders. The surplus, in men and materials, was assembled at the vast training centre at Tlemcen, through which thousands of Angolans and others have passed. Mr Chou En-lai, the Chinese Premier, naturally dropped in on his visit to Algeria early in 1964, was greatly impressed by what he saw, and made a substantial offer of help.

I know neither the size of the offer nor whether Mr Ben Bella accepted it. But it seems likely that it was indeed large and that it was accepted. Already in 1963, the Chinese government was offering to pay for the travelling expenses of Rhodesian nationalists who wished to travel to Tlemcen for training. This at any rate was what a delegate of ZANU (Rhodesia's Zimbabwe African National Union) who visited Algeria that year reported after his trip. President Ben Bella, he said, had offered free training in guerrilla warfare for Rhodesian Africans. (Ben Bella's successor, President Boumedienne, was less generous with the amenities of Tlemcen, though he, too, was ready to welcome Rhodesian Africans after Mr Ian Smith had proclaimed Rhodesia's independence.)

Travelling expenses to Tlemcen, however, can have been only a drop in the ocean of China's subversive effort in Africa, as a few more examples, chosen at random will show:

August 1963: two groups of Portuguese African rebels were on a guerrilla course in China. Some belonged to the African Independence Party of Guinea and the Cape Verde Islands (PAIGC, from the Portuguese); the others belonged to the Popular Movement for the Liberation of Angola (MPLA).

September 5, 1964: the Nairobi *East African Standard* reported that eighteen Kenyans were at Wuhan Military Academy, in China, on a guerrilla warfare course.

October 1964: an attempted uprising against President Diori of Niger was crushed. The President declared that the ringleaders had been trained in China.

December 1964: China offered scholarships for military training and other subjects to 'revolutionary' students in Indonesia—another example of three-cornered subversion, in line with the China–Rhodesia–Algeria case mentioned above. During the same month, the first batch of Luo tribe saboteurs and guerrillas returned to Kenya from China.

These examples could be multiplied indefinitely. But I have said enough to indicate what President Diori of Niger meant when he and President Yaméogo of Upper Volta on February 2, 1965, jointly condemned China's attempt to force 'ideology, weapons, money and subversion' into Africa. A few days earlier, President Houphouët-Boigny of the Ivory Coast, the 'father' of a whole generation of French-speaking African politicians, had put it in these words:

> The dangers threatening Africa today are those from communist China. . . . To reach their goal more rapidly, they have set up training camps for our African patriots from which communist subversion is organised to gnaw at our continent bit by bit. They have trained groups to be used to fight brothers and sisters in opposing camps. This is new in Africa and it is a tragedy that causes us anxiety.

The French-speaking Presidents were discovering what the English-speaking Dr Banda had already discovered. The language barrier is no bar to subversion in Africa.

3
Free for All

DURING the early 1960s, a curious notion gained currency in western capitals, that there were 'goodies' and 'baddies' in the communist world. The Chinese were clearly 'baddies', and since they were quarrelling with the Russians, the Russians began to look like 'goodies'. This theory, to which Sir Alec Douglas-Home, the Conservative Foreign Secretary and Prime Minister, appeared to subscribe, took various forms. It was argued, for instance, that 'fat' communists were better than 'lean' ones. The well-fed Russians were fatter (and better) than the leaner Chinese. The vituperative Chinese theoreticians fed the theory with their contemptuous references to Khrushchev's 'goulash communism'.

It was, I suppose, only human to wish to believe such things. Most of us are against war and poverty. The Russians were richer than the Chinese and seemed to be a good deal less warlike. It was tempting to deduce that there was a connection between their increasing affluence and their evident desire to avoid the general annihilation of nuclear war, and to argue that it was in the enlightened self-interest of the West to help the Russians—with loans or credits—to become fatter still and still more peace-loving.

Tempting, but illogical. The Russians were 'fatter' than the Chinese in 1956, when they massacred Hungarians for the crime of wanting to be neutral. It is, of course, not impossible that in time, Russia's communist rulers will become softer, more *embourgeoisés*, as the French put it, than they are now. Perhaps, if this ever happens, they will also drop the label 'communist' and allow rival political parties to compete for political power in the Soviet Union. Things as strange as this have happened before in politics. Let us, however, wait until this actually does happen before deciding that the Russians have become the 'goodies' of the world communist movement. For my part, I prefer to take notice of the things the Russians are doing, rather than the things they say. Their actions seem to show that fat communists are still, on the whole, as dangerous and meddlesome as lean ones. Moreover, as we have seen earlier in this book, the Soviet and Chinese positions on war are actually a good deal closer than is popularly supposed.

The Congo provides as good an illustration as any of the variety of subversive techniques to which the Russians are prepared to resort to gain control of a key African country. In June 1960, when the Congo became independent, Khrushchev must have felt that conditions were particularly favourable for a communist take-over. The Sino-Soviet dispute, though progressing behind the scenes, had not yet become an open split: broadly speaking, the communist powers were all pulling in the same direction. Patrice Lumumba, the erratic but spellbinding Prime Minister, had many communist friends and looked like proving malleable if inconsistent material. The Belgian Communist Party—still at that time a reliable instrument of Soviet policy—was in on the ground floor, as it were, having provided the new government with 'technical advisers'. Better still from a communist standpoint, the new State's embryonic army, the Belgian-trained Force Publique, mutinied so that law and order broke down, creating the classic preconditions for communist revolution.

This was the signal for the Soviet Union to start a massive airlift to the Congo. Food and medical supplies were certainly sent, but the main object of the airlift was to introduce arms and communist agents, and to put aircraft and lorries at Lumumba's disposal. When the United Nations decided to intervene, the Russians represented their airlift as a contribution to UN operations, while publicly attempting to discredit the UN for what it was trying to do. The build-up of agents was reflected in the swollen lists of Soviet and Czech embassy personnel in Leopoldville. On September 5, 1960, the

London *Times* reported that the two embassies between them had at least 200 diplomats and 'technicians' in the Congo, not counting medical teams. The experienced Soviet ambassador, Mikhael Yakovlev, was on close terms with Lumumba. The hour of the take-over must have seemed near.

A few days later, however, it all ended in fiasco. The cautious but wily President Kasavubu, leader of the Bakongo tribe and the descendant, it is said of a Chinese indentured labourer, dismissed Lumumba. This was on September 5. On September 14, Colonel Mobutu, the army's Commander-in-Chief, announced that the army was taking over and that the communist embassies had 40 hours to get out of the country. During the next day and night, large bonfires of presumably incriminating documents were seen in the grounds of the Soviet and Czech embassies. And on the 17th, the entire staffs of both embassies left Leopoldville by air.

Mobutu later explained why the Russians and Czechs had been turned out. A Soviet radio transmitter, he said, had been operating from the capital, where the Russians had set up a spy ring. The Russians, too, were behind an underground organisation charged with infiltrating Katanga, the Congo's richest province, and sabotaging mining and other installations there. Lumumba's brief-case, which he had left at an army camp where he had gone to plead with Colonel Mobutu to change his mind, also provided interesting evidence in the form of various letters and documents later published by the Congolese authorities. Unfortunately, some of these documents were forgeries. But among the ones which nobody, to my knowledge, has contested, were two that are of relevance to this chapter. One was a letter signed by Lumumba and addressed to the Soviet Union, asking for troops, planes, lorries and other supplies. The other was a letter from Chou En-lai, the Chinese Prime Minister, offering Lumumba's government £1 million.

Though expelled from Leopoldville, the Russians came in again by the back door of Stanleyville, when Antoine Gizenga, who had been Lumumba's right-hand man, went there and proclaimed himself Prime Minister after that unfortunate man's death in February 1961. And they were back in Leopoldville itself after Mr Cyrille Adoula had set up a generally recognised government there in August 1961, in which Gizenga took the post of deputy premier. But in October Gizenga broke away again, so the Soviet and other communist embassies tried to have it both ways: by keeping their diplomats accredited to Leopoldville, while flying arms and advisers—both military and technical—to Stanleyville.

It was perhaps not surprising when, in November 1963, the entire staff of the Soviet embassy in Leopoldville were expelled, for the second time in three years. Since the formation of the Adoula government, they had built up a mission with a personnel of nearly a hundred—far larger than the legitimate needs of Soviet representation could justify.

The incident that sparked their expulsion *en masse* was the discovery of papers on two Soviet diplomats, Boris Voronin and Yuri Myatkotnikh, which were said to prove that they had been plotting with the Congolese 'government-in-exile' in Brazzaville. This self-styled body was set up by the leaders of the left-wing Conseil National de Libération, which we met in the last chapter. These men, André Lubaya and Christophe Gbenye, had fled to the capital of the ex-French Congo in October after an abortive *coup d'état*. At a press conference on November 21, Mr Adoula claimed that the papers found on the two Russians included requests from Mr Gbenye to the Soviet embassy to provide weapons, tape recorders and counterfeit money. (Myatkotnikh, one of the two diplomats, had been found bribing delegates to the National Congress of the Congolese Student's Union in August 1963.)

On November 26, *Le Progrès* of Leopoldville printed the full text of the alleged documents. This showed that, in addition to the items mentioned by Mr Adoula, the Congolese rebels had asked the Russians to give travelling facilities to the Soviet Union for 'our young militants', and to provide miniature pistols in the form of cigarette lighters and fountain-pens, and double-bottomed suitcases.

Among other Congolese politicians who joined the 'government-in-exile' were Pierre Mulele, a former Education Minister in Lumumba's government (whom we met in the last chapter) and Anicet Kashamura, another former Lumumbist minister. No sooner was the 'government-in-exile' set up in Brazzaville than its members began to squabble with each other about whether to accept Chinese or Soviet advice and money. Mulele who, as we have seen, is reported to have undergone a course of training in guerrilla warfare in China, appears to have headed the pro-Chinese faction. At the end of January 1964, Mulele launched an armed rebellion in the Kwilu province of the former Belgian Congo. The central government announced that documents containing plans for the revolt included a translation of Mao Tse-tung's works on guerrilla warfare.

Up to this point, the evidence suggests that the Russians had been advocating a Soviet-style 'liberation' by means of a *coup d'état*, and that the rebels turned to Chinese-style methods—a peasant uprising—when the attempted coup failed. The Russians, however, seem to have felt that they could not afford to dissociate themselves from a liberation movement that was following Chinese advice. After hesitating awhile, Moscow radio came out in favour of Mulele's movement, which *Pravda* of February 11, 1964, praised as a patriotic uprising.

About that time a consignment of Russian and Czech arms, said to have been on its way to the Kwilu rebels, was stopped between Brazzaville and Leopoldville. This was not, indeed, the first evidence of an arms traffic between these facing Congolese capitals. On January 17, Mr Adoula called a press conference at his home to announce that a consignment of Soviet and Czech arms had been seized. Photographs of these weapons, which included rifles and sub-machine guns, were reproduced, together with fuller details, in *L'Etoile du Congo* the following day.

Towards the end of the year, there was evidence that foreign intervention in the Congo was becoming a free for all. Algerian and UAR planes started airlifting arms to the Congolese rebels, landing at Juba in the Sudan, whence supplies were overlanded to the eastern Congo. More supplies were being offloaded from ships of various nationalities at Dar-es-Salaam in the east and Pointe-Noire (Congo-Brazzaville) in the west.

In Leopoldville, the Congolese Commander-in-Chief, General (as he now was) Mobutu, gave some details of the airlift. On December 15, he said, ten UAR planes had landed at Juba, unloading arms and supplies for rebels, who at that time were regrouping not far away in the Aba area of the Congo. There had been twelve earlier flights which formed part of a regular, organised airlift by Egyptians, Algerians and others. Algerian instructors and field-doctors had also been flown to the Congolese border, added General Mobutu. Besides the Algerians and Egyptians, at least two other African countries were joining in the fun of aiding the Congolese insurgents. It is hard, otherwise, to see why a Malian plane and two Ghanaian ones had also found it necessary to land at the now curiously busy airport of Juba.

How far were the Russians involved in this arms-running? It is hard to say. What is certain is that the arms delivered by air from Algeria and Egypt were of Russian and Czech origin, and that the planes that delivered them were Russian-built AN 12 transports. We do not, however, have to depend on General Mobutu for proof of the charge that the Algerians and Egyptians were airlifting arms to the Congo, for Presidents Ben Bella and Nasser boasted of it. The latter, for instance, told a cheering crowd at Port Said on December 23: 'We do not conceal but openly say that we have sent arms to the Congo—and we shall send more'.

The Sudanese share in this operation is also not without interest. General Abboud, who seized power in the Sudan in 1958, had resolutely refused to allow Sudanese territory to be used as a staging point for arms deliveries. In October 1964,

72

however, the Abboud Government was overthrown after student demonstrations in which the police were misguided enough to open fire. The small but well organised Sudanese Communist Party was behind the demonstrations, and skilfully exploited public feeling against the authorities. As a reward, four Communists were included in the civilian administration of Serr el Khatem el Khalifa in November. The Khalifa government promptly reversed Abboud's stand on staging rights, and the airlift began.*

As it happens, the change of government in the Sudan roughly coincided with the overthrow of Khruschchev in Moscow. If one assumes, as I think one must, Soviet complicity in the Algerian-Egyptian airlift of arms to the Congolese rebels, one is entitled, at the minimum, to draw the conclusion that Khrushchev's successors, Kosygin and Brezhnev, are not less militant than he was. More than that one cannot say for certain, since it is quite possible that Khrushchev would have liked to provide facilities for an arms lift but was frustrated by Abboud's refusal of staging rights. Unlike Nasser and Ben Bella, the Soviet Premier, Kosygin, has not actually *boasted* of Soviet aid to the Congolese rebels. But the balance of probability is surely that the Soviet leaders didn't feel they could let the Chinese and the more militant Africans claim the sole credit for helping revolutionaries.

* * *

The Russians and Chinese are not, in any case, the only non-African communists engaged in subversion in various parts of Africa. The Bulgarians, whose ruling Communist Party is closer to Moscow than several others parties in eastern Europe, are particularly active. Details are known of a training course in violent subversion, which took place in Bulgaria in 1963. Some 200 Africans attended, among them 76 Kenyans and 15 Cameroonians. Trainees were taught how to make and

* The airlift petered out after a further change of government in June 1965.

throw bombs, or dispose of them in vulnerable places, and how to use small arms. Language was no problem: the instructors used English. That the course was part of a long-term plan was shown by the parting directive to 'lie low', cultivate friendships within the army, and await instructions.

Exiled left-wing organisations, including the UPC (which we met in the last chapter) lured Cameroonians to Bulgaria by promising them 'scholarships'. It was only later that they learned that this academic-sounding offer was valid for military training only. Fifteen made the trip to Bulgaria, and six of them were arrested when they returned.

Among these trainees was a Zambian who acquired some notoriety. Arrested at Ndola in December 1964, he was fined £45 with the option of seven months' gaol, for illegally importing arms and ammunition. His name was John Chanda, and his case was curious. When challenged by the police, he produced a 'certificate of origin' given to him by the Bulgarians, and claimed the weapons were presents from Bulgaria 'to show my party'. He seemed proud of the fact that the Bulgarians had given him the 'rank' of General, and corresponding 'perks' including well-appointed quarters and an official car.

Another 'Bulgarian' graduate rewarded with similar status symbols was Hiram Mwangi, a Kenyan whose name got into the papers in March 1963 as chief of a band of young guerrilla fighters. An earlier 'graduate' of Bulgaria's school of subversion, he was one of a group of three Kenyans who left for Bulgaria late in 1961.

Czechoslovakia and East Germany are also involved in the training of Africans for subversion, though whether this training extends to guerrilla warfare is obscure. More active than either in this respect is distant Cuba, which enjoyed two rare advantages, in comparison with the East European countries (though not with China)—a surplus of battle-hardened guerrilla fighters and a leading theoretician of guerrilla warfare, the Argentine-born Major Ernesto 'Che' Guevara, Fidel Castro's Minister of Industries until March 1965, when he vanished in unexplained circumstances. One of Cuba's leading 'industries' is, in fact, the training of revolutionaries, for export to continental Latin America and elsewhere; so it was perhaps appropriate that the island's Minister of Industries should have been the author of the well-known manual, *La Guerra de Guerrillas.*

Africans from Zanzibar and Kenya, from South Africa and Rhodesia, from Angola, Mali and Ghana have been through Cuba's main revolutionary training camp at Minas del Frío, appropriately sited on the slopes of the Sierra Maestra, where Fidel Casto defied the dictator Batista, and occasionally fought him until the collapse of the dictatorship cleared the way for a triumphal entry into Havana. The Guerrilla Academy, as the establishment at Minas del Frío is known, provides the military and practical aspects of a training course whose theoretical and political sides are taught at Havana.

Most of the 'undergraduates' at Cuba's Guerrilla Academy are, of course, Latin Americans from various countries; and we shall deal with this aspect of the struggle for the Third World in the fourth section of this book. When one considers how far Cuba is from Africa, and how great and vicious is Cuba's effort in Latin America, it is remarkable that the Cubans manage to make space for between 100 and 200 Africans a year in their Guerrilla Academy. The Cubans, however, are successful revolutionaries, who know what they are doing. How important the revolutionary industry was to Fidel Castro's Minister of Industries emerged when Major Guevara made a six-week tour of African States in December and January, 1964–65. It was not necessary, said Guevara in Ghana, to export revolution; all that was needed was to give practical support to all revolutionary movements. 'Africa', he declared, 'contains more revolutionary ferment than most people would believe.'

The fact is that, according to Cuban revolutionary doctrine —of which Guevara was a leading exponent—the processing and re-export of revolutionaries is a highly productive investment. Large numbers are not needed: twenty or thirty highly trained men can spark a revolution, or seize control of it, given money and arms or explosives, and a local situation of resentment against a tyranny. We shall see in time how this theory was applied to the revolutionary situation in the Dominican Republic in the spring of 1965. What interests us here is how it was applied in Zanzibar in January 1964.

The tiny new State of Zanzibar, off the east coast of Africa, famous for its cloves and trade winds, had not long been independent. In the small hours of January 12, a band of rebels broke into the armoury and helped themselves to its contents, seized the main police station and the radio station and deposed the Sultan. Essentially, this was a racial uprising of Africans against an Arab-dominated government, as the piled-up corpses of Arabs in the streets demonstrated. Its details need not concern us. The relevant thing, in this chapter, is that twenty or thirty Zanzibaris, trained in Cuba, formed the spearhead of the revolt.

The ostensible leader of the revolt, previously unknown but soon to enjoy a brief flash of notoriety, was not a Zanzibari at all but a personage calling himself 'Field-Marshal' John Okello, formerly a Mau Mau terrorist in Kenya but originally a Langi tribesman from Uganda. Okello, however, was merely an uncouth pawn in the hands of a mustachioed, gap-toothed, smiling, bravado-dispensing 'journalist' called Abdul Rahman Mohammed Babu, who had been the local correspondent of the New China News Agency (Hsinhua). In January 1962 —well in advance of any independence time-table, Babu had sent Okello and more than two score Zanzibaris to Cuba for a full two-year course in revolutionary military methods. *His* timing was perfect, and his twenty or thirty Cuban-trained revolutionaries were on hand when the hour of action struck.

Perhaps the most interesting aspect of this miniature take-over bid was the extent to which the Communist parties of various countries cooperated to ensure that the impending anti-Asian and anti-Arab revolt in Zanzibar should come under communist control. As we have seen, Babu had links with Peking as well as Havana. In fact, a number of Babu's supporters were trained in Peking and some in Prague (under the auspices of the World Federation of Trade Unions); and communist agents from several countries are believed to have met in Leningrad, Prague, Sofia and Warsaw as early as 1962 (when Babu's men were being trained in Cuba) to discuss plans for the revolt. This cooperation is an important, as well as an interesting, fact, for its meaning is clear: whatever the doctrinal differences within the world communist movement, and even though the movement is no longer a reliable instrument of Soviet foreign policy, the parties in power are united in working for revolution.

To say, as Guevara and Chou En-lai have said, that they do not export revolution is a quibble. Nor is there much consolation to be derived from the fact that the Chinese and Russians are competing—not cooperating—with one another in their revolutionary endeavours. In fact, if not in theory, their subversive actions are complementary.

The union of Tanganyika and Zanzibar to form the Republic of Tanzania has, of course, blurred the picture and it is hard to say whether the communists have been deprived of their chance to gain complete control of Zanzibar, or given a chance to gain control of Tanzania as a whole. (Babu, who was Foreign Minister in Zanzibar's military regime, became Tanzania's Minister for Commerce and Cooperatives.) Certainly President Nyerere, no communist despite his deceptively mild-mannered militancy, has given signs of awareness of the dangers of subversion. In November 1964, for instance, his government decided to cut down the personnel of 'liberation' offices in Dar-es-Salaam to four apiece and to transfer surplus members to Mbeyan, more than 300 miles inland, on the ground that they would be less able to stir up trouble there and foreign diplomats less able to subvert them.

* * *

The Zanzibar revolt of January 1964 was followed within a few days by mutinies in the armies of Tanganyika, Uganda and Kenya. How far communist agents were implicated in these affairs is still obscure. More of the truth has come to light in Kenya than elsewhere. As early as 1962, when Babu's Zanzibaris were in Cuba, groups of young Kenyans were being trained in the Soviet Union and Ghana in sabotage and guerrilla warfare. They were to come back, form 'action brigades' and seize power by force when independence came.

Why Ghana? To answer this question would be to probe the complex mind of Kwame Nkrumah, President of Ghana. Dr Nkrumah's pan-African aspirations are, of course, well-known, and they are supposed to be served by the African Affairs Bureau in Accra. Unfortunately, communists of many shades infest the offices of the Bureau. Name a dissident African movement and you will almost certainly find it represented there. Many of these movements are more or less communist, for instance the Cameroonian UPC, the Nigerian Sawaba, Senegal's Parti Africain de l'Indépendance and Ivory Coast's Sanwi.

The Bureau publishes *The Spark* (which was also the name of Lenin's paper: *Iskra* in Russian) and the young Marxists who run it, and have Nkrumah's ear, are closely connected with the British Communist Party. Russians and Poles, East Germans and communists from France, Italy and the United States jostle with African nationalists in the African Affairs Bureau. Perhaps this explains a report that a guerrilla training camp exists on Ghanaian soil. There, it is said, young Kenyans were trained in revolutionary violence, for use in their own country.

The implications of subversive training in Ghana and in the communist countries were seen in focus when it was learnt, towards the end of 1964, that communist planes had been secretly flying arms into Kenya. On March 30, 1965, the Defence Minister, Dr Njoroge Mungai, told Parliament that:

'Many people have been trained in the armed forces of other countries, and the first we know about it is when they get back'.

On April 2, a backbencher, Mr Tom Malinda, caused a stir when he declared that he would produce evidence to show that 'arms and ammunition are being smuggled continuously from communist and other countries into or through Kenya for the purpose of staging an armed revolution to overthrow our beloved government, or involving us in external conflict'.

These statements were in fact signs of a great Kenyan awakening to the dangers of communist subversion. A wave of indignation had swept the country early in April when twenty-nine students, returning after only a few months in the Soviet Union, described the hardships, racial discrimination and political indoctrination they had encountered during their 'studies'. Their return approximately coincided with the opening of the first course at the new Lumumba Institute.

The Russians must have thought the Institute would be a major instrument of their policy in Kenya. They had met half the building costs, and part of the rest had come from the communist-controlled International Organisation of Journalists. There were two Russians on the staff, and seven Kenyans who had been trained in Moscow.

The purpose of the Institute was not, however, to propagate communism but to train members of the ruling Kenya African National Union (KANU) in government, in the framework of African Socialism. From the first, the communists at the Institute, and some of their friends outside, including the Vice-President, Oginga Odinga, had tried to argue that African Socialism and communism (described as 'scientific socialism') were one and the same.

On April 27, however, the government rejected this view in a White Paper which drew a sharp distinction between African Socialism and communism. And the National Assembly placed the Institute under the control of the Ministry of Education, where, some may think, it should have been all along.

The Institute row coincided with the even more spectacular affair of the Soviet arms. President Kenyatta himself went to Mombasa docks as a Soviet arms ship berthed, declared the arms to be 'old and second-hand and of no use to Kenya's modern army' and sent them back to Russia. One suspects that obsolescence was the least of the drawbacks he saw in accepting so potentially explosive a gift from the Russians. This impression was strengthened on June 1 when President Kenyatta, watching a parade of the armed forces in Nairobi, roundly denounced communist subversion. Forty-eight hours earlier Vice-President Odinga had denounced British and American imperialism in even stronger terms. But Odinga's star was waning, for two days after the President's speech the Vice-President was deprived of the honour of leading Kenya's delegation to the Commonwealth Prime Ministers' conference in London. Kenya had woken up.

* * *

If this were a thesis for a Ph.D., I should feel obliged to describe communist efforts to take over the anti-Portuguese movements in Angola, Mozambique and Portuguese Guinea; to analyse the ups and downs of Soviet policy in Guinea; and to say something of China's massive effort to subvert Mali. But this is a Background Book and there are other parts of the world to be dealt with, the struggle for the Third World being world-wide. But enough has been said, I suggest, to show the nature of the new scramble for Africa and to demonstrate that the people who count least in communist calculations throughout the continent are the Africans themselves.

III

Asia's Hot Cold War

I

Subversion in Perspective

THE HISTORY of communist subversion in South-East Asia and the Far East is long, tortuous and bloody. In this region more than anywhere else, the cold war has tended to be 'hot', erupting in a series of insurrections, riots and local wars. It is not part of my purpose to go over this history in any detail (I retraced it in my Penguin Special, *South-East Asia in Turmoil*), but a few essential things have to be stated if the present phase (which does concern us) is to be understood.

Although a Communist Party was set up in South Africa as early as 1921, the Russians were more intensely interested in the Far East in those early years than in any other part of what was later to be known as the Third World. Lenin thought he could hasten the 'inevitable' collapse of western capitalism by helping the colonial peoples throw off the shackles of imperialism, thereby depriving the 'imperialists' of raw materials. This was his main object in setting up the Comintern, or Communist International, in 1919. During the next ten years, a number of Communist parties were established in Asia: in Indonesia—then the Dutch East Indies (1920)—China (1921), India (1925) and Indochina (1930). The communists tried to set up Soviet States in Indonesia, Singapore and the Philippines; but these early essays in revolution all came to grief and their leaders were gaoled.

The Second World War gave the Soviet communists and their Asian agents fresh opportunities. Between December 1941 and the middle of 1942, the Japanese armies overran Malaya, Singapore, Burma, the Dutch East Indies and the Philippines, setting up indirect rule in Siam and French Indochina. At first, the local nationalists greeted the Japanese as liberators; later, disillusioned by Japanese behaviour, they set up resistance movements in the jungles and mountains. In all these movements, the local communists played an important part. This indeed was what they had been waiting for: a chance to identify themselves with the nationalists. In Malaya and the Philippines, the communists actually achieved the leadership of the anti-Japanese resistance. In Burma and Indonesia, they merely participated in it, among others.

The suddenness of the Japanese collapse in August 1945 took everybody by surprise. The returning allies were late in reaching Malaya and Indonesia, and in the former the communists initiated a reign of terror and tried to set up a people's democracy. Much the same thing happened in the Philippines while General MacArthur was reconquering the main island of Luzon.

Stalin had dissolved the Comintern during the war, and many people had concluded (as he intended them to) that the idea of world revolution had been abandoned. The Comintern, however, was revived in 1947 under a new name: the Cominform. The late Zhdanov, then Stalin's right-hand man, master-minded a new plan for revolution throughout South-East Asia in 1948. In that year, the communists duly launched insurrections in India, Malaya, Burma, the Philippines and Indonesia. About eighteen months earlier, the Vietnamese communists had independently launched an insurrection against the French, which culminated in the loss of France's Indochina empire. The other communist insurrections, however, all either collapsed or drifted on inconclusively.

From 1959, the ideological rift between Peking and Moscow began to have embarrassing effects on the Communist parties of East Asia. Some of them—in particular those of India and Japan—split into pro-Soviet and pro-Chinese wings. Others —such as those of North Vietnam and Indonesia—decided, with reservations, to side with China, the giant neighbour on the doorstep. The Russians, on their side, have fought hard to restore their position as leaders of the world communist movement, in Asia as elsewhere.

As these lines were written, in mid-1965, the struggle for South-East Asia was no longer a simple matter of East versus West, of communism versus nationalism, or even of Peking versus Moscow. Certainly these elements were all present. But there were complicating factors as well, such as the irredentist ambitions of the North Vietnamese communist leader, Ho Chi Minh; and the increasing power and independence of the Indonesian Communist Party (PKI). Over everything, there weighed the crushing presence of China.

Perhaps the struggle can best be understood in terms of the *aims* of the forces, movements or Powers involved in it, starting with the major crises of Vietnam and Malaysia. In Vietnam, the North Vietnamese communists were trying to evict the Americans and establish their rule, not only over the whole of Vietnam but also over the neighbouring countries of Laos and Cambodia. The Chinese were looking on, shouting encouragement from the sidelines, but obviously unwilling to joint in for fear of a direct clash with the United States. The Russians had no more taste than the Chinese for confrontation with the Americans, but felt they had to do something— preferably not much—to help the North Vietnamese, partly to compete with the Chinese, and partly to gain a place of importance at any peace conference. In Indonesia's confrontation with Malaysia, the running was made by President Sukarno of Indonesia, whose objectives in the area were to get rid of the British and the Americans, in that order. The PKI (Indonesian Communists) were using the situation to strengthen their own position. Here again, the Chinese communists were shouting encouragement, but their main interest seemed to be to build up solidarity with Indonesia, in order to oust the Russians from the Afro-Asian movement. As for the Russians, they were providing Sukarno's forces with the arms to do the job. In Malaysia itself, the mainly Chinese communist movement was busy with anti-Malaysia subversion; and the activities of the Malayan Communist Party extended to Siam.

Elsewhere in Asia, the struggle for influence was continuing.

In Burma, the pro-Chinese communists were working for the violent overthrow of General Ne Win's military and socialist regime, while the pro-Russian communists were trying to subvert it by infiltrating into the administration. In India, the pro-Chinese communists had tried to facilitate China's aggression of 1962, while it suited the Russians to let the Indians think they were India's friends. In Nepal and Ceylon, too, competitive subversion was at work, while in Japan, China's objective was to rouse public opinion against America, and Russia's dilemma was how to counter China's efforts without seeming pro-American.

Among all these anti-western, or anti-nationalist, or mutually antagonistic objectives, one thing was absent on the communist side: any concern for the welfare, stability or happiness of the peoples of South-East Asia.

2

The Trouble-makers: North Vietnam

THE TEMPTATION to see China's hidden hand behind everything that goes wrong in South-East Asia is strong indeed. Often enough, as we shall see, the Chinese *are* behind situations of chaos and disorder. But paradoxically, there is less evidence of Chinese trouble-making on China's own doorstep than far away in Africa. It is as though the Chinese communists are so confident that their size and position will prove decisive in the end that they are content to let history take its course in South-East Asia.

This is admittedly an oversimplification. But the fact is that in a number of situations, events have been going very nicely for them, without the need for any great effort on their part. Two such situations are those of Indochina and Malaysia, where, in effect, others are doing the 'dirty' work. In Indochina, the principal trouble-maker is not Mao Tse-tung, but the Vietnamese communist leader, Ho Chi Minh. In the Indonesia-Malaysia 'confrontation', the trouble-maker of course has been President Sukarno, who is not a communist but—like Nasser and Ben Bella in northern Africa—was in alliance with the communists, who were exploiting the situation for all it was worth. It was not, of course, worth the same to the Russian communists as to the Chinese, or to the Chinese as to the Indonesians. So in a sense this was an example in action of the old communist slogan: from each according to his work to each according to his needs.

Let us start, then, with Ho Chi Minh. This extraordinary man, one of the leading revolutionaries of Asia and the world, is a nationalist as well as a communist, and in that simple fact lies the clue to his complex character. His first aim in life was the anti-colonial one of dislodging the French from Indo-china, and he turned to communism, as many other Asian and African revolutionaries did in the 1920s, because at that time the communists appeared to be the only dedicated opponents of colonialism.

His real name is Nguyen That Thanh, and it is characteristic of him that he later chose for himself the *nom de guerre* of Nguyen Ai Quoc, or Nguyen the Patriot. His present and universally known nickname means 'the one who sheds enlightenment' and he has stuck to it although it was originally given to him as a jest by Chinese prison guards when he was gaoled in China in 1942.

The fact that Ho is a nationalist does not, however, mean that his communism is insincere. He is indeed a convinced and life-long communist; but he has used communism, as Mao has used it, to serve his nationalist aims. He was a founder member of the French Communist Party in 1920, graduated as a revolutionary from Moscow's University of Toilers of the East, turned up in Canton in 1925 as assistant to Russia's chief agent in South China, Michael Borodin, and founded a communist group in Siam in 1928. But his career, for the purposes of this book, really begins in 1930.

At that time, Ho was in Hong Kong. As a nationalist committed to communism, he lacked a reliable instrument for the fulfilment of his own ambitions. Vietnam was not short of Communist parties. That was just the trouble: there were three of them and mutually hostile. So Ho summoned dele-gates of all three parties to Hong Kong, where his patience and natural authority welded them into a single party under his leadership.

It was at this stage that Ho Chi Minh first revealed, albeit indirectly, the territorial extent of his ambitions. When the new united party was founded, in March 1930, it was called *Vietnam Cong San Dang*, or *Vietnam* Communist Party. But in October, its name was changed to *Dong Duong Cong San Dang*, or *Indochina* Communist Party. A small change, you might think, but a deeply significant one. At that time, French Indochina consisted of Laos, Cambodia and Vietnam (itself divded into the three *ky* or provinces of Tonkin, Annam and Cochinchina). Accidents of history had united these three countries under French rule, but each was inhabited by a distinct people, with a language, culture and history of its own. Traditionally, the more energetic and expansive Vietnamese had encroached on their neighbours' territory. By changing the name of his new party to cover activities in neighbouring territories as well as his own, Ho was giving notice that he intended to carry on the interventionist tradition. Today, in the retrospect of thirty-five years, it can be clearly seen that he has never wavered in his intention of extending Vietnamese rule over Laos and Cambodia. Today, as these lines were being written, Ho was 75. He controlled much of Laos and South Vietnam, though he was losing ground. Cambodia escaped him but his southern guerrillas were using Cambodian territory to rest, train and flee when pursued by American and South Vietnam forces. But for one thing—American power—the irredentist dream of thirty-five years ago would be on the point of coming true.

The preceding paragraph may sound like supposition, but it is based on solid fact. All the artifices and techniques of communist subversion—from mystification and the 'front' method to terrorism and revolutionary war—have been used by Ho in his drive for power over his own and neighbouring lands. Even a bare recital of facts and dates is illuminating:

1941: Vietnam Independence League (*Vietminh*) formed as ostensibly nationalist alliance between communists and other anti-French parties.

1945: Indochina Communist Party 'dissolves' itself. This was part of the mystification process. Ho's Democratic Republic of Vietnam had just been proclaimed. By 'dissolving' his party (whose organisation, in fact, remained intact), Ho was trying to give the impression that the Vietnamese had dropped any designs on neighbouring countries, and to make Vietnamese nationalists believe that their communist allies had opted out of the world communist movement.

1946: Formation of Vietnam People's United Front (*Lien Viet*), with the hidden object of bringing all sectors of Vietnam's population under the control of the apparently dissolved Communist Party.

1951: Communist Party re-emerges under the name of Vietnam Workers' Party (Vietnam *Lao Dong Dang*). By this time most of the non-communist nationalists had left the Vietminh and there was no point in pretending that there was no Communist Party. The term 'Indochina' was still dropped, however, as a disclaimer of irredentism. But this was a hollow pretence, for as soon as the new party had been formed, delegates from two shadow bodies—the People's United Fronts of Cambodia and Laos—took part in a joint conference with the Lien Viet. From this emerged a Joint National United Front for the whole of Indochina. This was supposed to justify military action in Laos and Cambodia by the Vietminh forces fighting the French. But in reality, it provided cover for Vietnamese communist designs on those two countries. This was conclusively by a secret directive of the Lao Dong party, dated November 1, 1951, and later captured by the French. This said the Communist Parties of Laos and Cambodia, though overtly under Laotian and Cambodian leadership, would continue to get orders from the 'dissolved' Indochina Party, and added: 'But later on, when conditions permit, . . . the three revolutionary parties of Vietnam, Cambodia and Laos will be reunited to form a single party.'

1953: Vietminh army invades Laos and sets up communist administration, known as Pathet Lao (Lao State), in two Laotian provinces.

1955: First evidence of the establishment of the Revolutionary Party (Pracheachon) of Cambodia. This seems to have taken the place of the clandestine Cambodian section of the old Indochina Party. In September the Lien Viet front was absorbed into a new Fatherland Front, charged with securing the reunification of Vietnam (which had been partitioned under the Geneva agreements that ended the first Indochina war).

1959: Lao Dong Central Committee decides to 'liberate' South Vietnam by force (May).

1960: Lao Dong Congress decides to set up United Front in South Vietnam (September). National Front for the Liberation of South Vietnam created (December).

1962: Creation of South Vietnamese People's Revolutionary Party. Captured documents have since identified this organisation as a subsidiary of the Lao Dong. In March, first mention of a parallel organisation for Laos, the Laotian People's Party (also known as Workers' Party), which had probably been in existence for several years. The leaders of this party, though Laotians, are also members of the Lao Dong party.

Though this chronology speaks for itself, it may gain from a few words of explanation. When the Vietminh army, thinly disguised as 'people's volunteers', overran two provinces of Laos in April 1953, they came with a self-proclaimed mission 'to make revolution in Cambodia and Laos' and 'build the union of Vietnam, Cambodia and Laos'. The Geneva settlement of 1954, to which the Vietnamese communists were a party, recognised the authority of the King of Laos over the whole of his kingdom, including the two provinces occupied by the communists. Despite further 'scraps of paper', however, the Vietnamese communists and their Laotian puppets never quite abandoned their hold on the territory seized in 1953.

In 1962, after a protracted international conference, again in Geneva, the neutrality and integrity of Laos were guaranteed by the participants, who included communist North Vietnam. The Lao agreement settled nothing however, mainly because some 5,000 Vietnamese communist troops remained behind after the agreed deadline for withdrawal of all foreign troops (October 7, 1962). A year after the 'settlement', each Pathet Lao battalion included forty to fifty Vietnamese communist 'technical experts' and eleven North Vietnamese regular battalions were deployed along the so-called 'Ho Chi Minh trail' leading from North to South Vietnam across Laotian territory. At the time of writing, there were probably well over 10,000 North Vietnamese troops in Laos.

There can be little doubt, in the light of the events recounted above, that should the Vietnamese communists gain control over the whole of Vietnam, they would absorb Laos as well. (Cambodia is also an objective, but would prove a tougher proposition.) For the present, however, their main interest in Laos is that it serves as a stepping stone to South Vietnam. Now the partition of Vietnam was not supposed to be permanent, for under the Final Declaration of the 1954 Geneva Conference, there was provision for the reunification of the country through general elections. The Final Declaration, however, unlike the purely military agreements between the French and Vietminh high commands, was unsigned; and the South Vietnamese and American governments publicly dissociated themselves from the settlement.

A new government—that of the late Ngo Dinh Diem—had taken office in South Vietnam shortly before agreement had been reached at Geneva. This government was not responsible for the war, for the French defeat, or for the truce agreement. It knew that whatever international safeguards were provided, elections could never be free in North Vietnam, and when the time came, refused to discuss election arrangements with the North.

Frustrated of the prize it considered rightfully its own, the Vietminh army, which had decisively defeated the French at Dien Bien Phu, decided to gain its objectives by a further dose of 'revolutionary war'. The communist Commander-in-Chief, General Vo Nguyen Giap, knew all about revolutionary war: he had studied it with the Chinese communists during China's civil war and adapted Mao's theories to Vietnam's special conditions during the first Indochina war against the French. Giap's tactics had proved extraordinarily successful against France and they have since proved equally successful against the South Vietnam government and its American allies.

Conditions were favourable for the communists when the second Indochina war began. The Diem regime had achieved a good deal between 1954 and 1957, resettling nearly a million refugees from the communist North, restoring rice production and defeating various challenges to its authority. It was essentially, however, an authoritarian family dictatorship and was unpopular, especially with two militant political and religious sects in Cochinchina—the Hoa Hao and Caodai. Towards the end of 1957, these sects took up arms against the central government, and they were soon joined by small groups of communist irregulars who had hidden the arms they had once used against the French.

Soon, the communists were in control of the insurrection. They moved into villages, terrorised the locals and murdered officials appointed by the government in Saigon. Rounding up young men, they would force these to join them in armed actions. Defectors were promptly executed; so were villagers misguided enough to let the authorities know where the guerrillas were hiding. In time, North Vietnam started supplying the Vietcong, as the communist guerrillas were known. Arms and ammunition were sent down from the North through the Laotian jungle, along what has come to be known as the Ho Chi Minh trail, by junk along the coast and by sampan on the Mekong river. As the guerrilla movement gathered strength, Hanoi began sending not only heavier arms, but also officers and men of the regular army.

As we have seen from the chronology of Vietnamese communist activities, the Lao Dong central committee decided to 'liberate' South Vietnam by force in 1959. To do this satisfactorily, from Hanoi's viewpoint, it was first necessary to establish a 'front' that would control the Vietcong guerrillas on the political side, and which would in turn, be controlled by the Communist Party. Hence the Lao Dong's decision of September 10, 1960, to set up a front in South Vietnam. The following January, Hanoi radio announced the creation the previous month of the National Front for the Liberation of South Vietnam (NFLSV).

In mid-1965, when these lines were written, much was being heard of the argument that the Americans—by then deeply involved in the second Indochina war—should negotiate a settlement with the NFLSV. It was argued that this was an autonomous body, by no means preponderantly communist, and that it was the true authority for South Vietnam. I have always found it hard to follow this argument, for in fact, the NFLSV was simply a branch office of the communist ruling party of North Vietnam, the Lao Dong. At first, indeed, the communists hardly bothered to make the Front look convincing. A Front, after all, even by communist definitions, implies a coalition of parties with political intent. Yet at first, the NFLSV represented only itself. Then, at intervals, Hanoi radio began announcing the formation of one party or organisation after another, all of which were said to belong to the NFLSV. Fourteen of these alleged bodies were announced, but it turned out that they shared the same officials. An 'overworked' man was Nguyen Van Hieu, who was described by Hanoi radio on April 16, 1962, as Secretary-General of the NFLSV and of two of the supposed components of the Front, the 'South Vietnam Committee for the Defence of World Peace' and the 'Radical Socialist Party'. Later he was being described as Vice-President of the 'Association of Patriotic and Democratic Journalists', in which capacity he had turned up in Budapest in August 1962. One wonders how Mr Hieu found time to fulfil all his functions.

In fact, only one party matters in the NFLSV: the Vietnamese People's Revolutionary Party, whose existence was not revealed until January 1962. In its inaugural manifesto, the PRP admitted that it was the successor of the Indochina Communist Party and of the Lao Dong; but captured documents have since made it plain that the PRP is simply a subsidiary of the Lao Dong. It takes its orders from Hanoi and transmits them to the NFLSV. In a way, this is a case of one 'Front' giving orders to another 'Front', for the real body that directs the national liberation war in South Vietnam is a direct offshoot of the Lao Dong's central committee, known as the 'Committee for Supervision of the South'. Another link in the elaborate chain of command is the massive Central Research Agency, which is Hanoi's intelligence service. Cowed by terrorism, the population of the South provides the Vietcong with an endless stream of information which the southern regular army and its American allies lack.

The fanaticism of the North Vietnamese communists, their years of preparation, their ruthlessness and their meticulous organisation have yielded dramatic successes. In 1959, there could hardly have been more than 3,000 communist guerrillas under arms in South Vietnam. By the spring of 1965, the hard core of the Vietcong consisted of 35,000 full-time battle-hardened guerrillas, supported by a further 70,000 or 80,000 auxiliary forces, who grew rice by day and fought by night. This, too, had been the pattern during the first Indochina war.

* * *

North Vietnam's activities in Cambodia are smaller in scale and less successful than in Laos or South Vietnam. A glance at a map of Indochina helps to explain why, but doesn't tell the whole story. As a country, Laos is weaker, poorer and less cohesive than Cambodia, and it was relatively easy for the Vietnamese communists to invade Laos and set up an administration subservient to their orders. They did set up a small resistance movement against the French in Cambodia during the first Indochina war, and tried hard to have it recognised at the Geneva conference of 1954. But the attempt came to nothing and—alone of the three Indochina States—Cambodia emerged from the conference with its territory intact. This was one advantage. Another was the dynamic leadership of Cambodia's Head of State, Prince Sihanouk, whose Popular Socialist Party has established a virtual monopoly of political power and driven both the communists and rebellious nationalists to despair or exile.

It must not be thought, however, that the Lao Dong has left Cambodia alone. The old aims of the Indochina Communist Party have been kept alive. In the spring of 1960, Prince Sihanouk wrote an article in his favourite mouthpiece, *The Nationalist*, complaining that the Vietminh (as he went on calling the Vietnamese communists) was trying to subvert Cambodia. To do this, he wrote, the Vietnamese were using their agents in the local Pracheachon (Revolutionary) party, which indeed the Vietminh had set up in 1955. He complained that a Vietminh agent, who had been arrested, was carrying documents that attacked him and his party. Other seized documents showed that the communists had ordered their agents to infiltrate the Popular Socialist Community in order to take over the direction of 'certain services' while waiting for the right moment to destroy the Community and the Cambodian monarchy (which Cambodia still was, although Prince Sihanouk had abdicated his throne). In May 1962, when fourteen members of the Pracheachon were sentenced to death for subversive activities, it was seen that Vietnamese communists had not allowed the Prince's earlier disclosures to interfere with their long-range plans for Cambodia.

3

The Trouble-makers: Indonesia

Ho Chi Minh's major competitor as a trouble-maker in South-East Asia is President Sukarno of Indonesia. But I don't propose to deal with his activities in any detail. What concerns us here is the use that has been made of his policy of 'confrontation' with Malaysia by his communist allies. In other words, the further trouble-making that has been stimulated by this leading trouble-maker's actions.

Nor do I propose to deal with the Malaysia issue as such, beyond a few words explaining my use of the slightly charged expression, 'trouble-maker'. Singapore's reluctant secession from the Malaysian Federation in August 1965 was naturally hailed in Djakarta as a victory. It was not an Indonesian victory, however, so much as a self-inflicted defeat by the Malaysians themselves who, in effect, had scored a goal against their own side. The unity of Singapore and Malaya (which together with the Borneo territories of Sarawak and Sabah constituted Malaysia) was shattered by communal tension between Malays and Chinese.

If communalism was a built-in problem of Malaysia, on the other hand, Indonesia's confrontation was an additional burden which it might well have been spared. It is, I think, self-evident that the young federation of 11 million inhabitants could not possibly be a threat to Indonesia's 103 million people. The confrontation crisis was, in fact, entirely of Sukarno's making, and that is why I call him a trouble-maker.

To think of communist trouble-making in the Malaysian-Indonesian area as a mere by-product of Sukarno's trouble-making would, however, be a mistake. The communists have, in fact, been at it much longer than Sukarno. But the present situation has been a windfall for them in various ways. For the PKI (Indonesia's Communist Party) it provided a chance to identify itself with Sukarno's nationalism, which it exploited with outstanding ability and daring. For the Chinese communist government and party it provided a handy issue with which to berate the 'imperialists' and neo-colonialists' in Asia, and to extend their influence over the PKI and Indonesia, the largest and most important country in South-East Asia.

For the Russians, too, the confrontation has been useful, since it has enabled them to 'prove', in the face of Peking's taunts and accusations, that they are as anti-imperialist' as anybody, and better able than others, say the Chinese, to help a revolutionary Afro-Asian government. It must be said, on the other hand, that the Malaysian crisis has been of doubtful value to Malaysia's local communists, most of whom are Chinese and whose opposition to Malaysia lays them open to the charge that they are simply furthering China's own imperialist aims. Moreover, the many 'overseas' Chinese in Malaysia and Singapore who have no wish to be ruled either by Sukarno or by Mao Tse-tung have no natural liking for the present rather unholy alliance between the predominantly Chinese communists of Malaysia and Malaysia's Indonesian enemies. They know, even if Malaysia's Chinese communists profess not to, that the Chinese community fares infinitely better in Malaysia than in Indonesia.

* * *

Turning now from Sukarno to the communist troublemakers, one must spare a few words for his runner-up in trouble-making, Dipa Nusantara Aidit, chairman of the PKI. Born in 1923 in Sumatra, Aidit claims to be of 'pure Malayan stock', despite allegations that he has Chinese or Arab blood. His second name—a Javanese term meaning 'outer world'—was used for nationalist purposes by anti-colonial Indonesians in the 1920s.

Until his fortunes changed in 1965 Aidit was very successful. To understand the degree of his success, one has to recall the condition of the PKI at the end of 1948. An ill-starred communist rebellion against the young Indonesian Republic, launched on Moscow's orders and without popular support, had been smashed by the Army, leaving the party leaderless and diminished. In 1952, the party's Politburo put the PKI membership at only 7,910 members. By the end of 1954— three years or so after Aidit had taken over the leadership— membership had grown to 500,000. Later, it was said to exceed 3 million.

Like most successful generals, D. N. Aidit had luck on his side, as well as ability. He had the luck to take over the broken PKI during the premiership of a Nationalist Party leader— Dr Ali Sastroamidjojo—who wanted the party to become strong again as a counterweight to his powerful Muslim political rivals. It was luck again that Sukarno himself decided he needed the PKI as a counterweight to the Army, after a major rebellion had broken out in 1958. One result of the 1958 rebellion was that two of the PKI's rivals, the Socialist and Masjumi (moderate Muslim) parties, were banned. This, too, was luck; and in 1960 came a further reward, when President Sukarno launched the slogan word NASAKOM (nationalism, religion and communism), recognising the PKI as one of the three main forces in Indonesian politics.

It was luck again, when the Malaysian issue turned up. The PKI was quick off the mark. In November 1961, agreement had been reached in London between Malaya and Britain that would lead to the formation of the Federation of Malaysia, and the Indonesian government had cautiously welcomed the news. But a month later, the PKI's central committee denounced 'the formation of a new concentration of colonial forces on the very frontiers of our country'. Aidit had the satisfaction of seeing this 'neo-colonialist' presentation of his case against Malaysia adopted *subsequently* by the Soviet and Chinese Communist Parties and by the Sukarno government.

Luck alone, however, would not account for the PKI's success under Aidit. Originally regarded as a 'Moscow' man—as distinct from his Number Two, Lukman, the 'Peking' man —Aidit, in fact, navigated with remarkable skill among the shoals of the Sino-Soviet dispute, while exploiting the party's 'nationalism' for all it was worth in Indonesian domestic politics. He followed Moscow's line of constitutional advance while overtly siding with Peking in the dispute; at the same time, he was speaking in favour of peasant insurrection and stirring up trouble among the sometimes famished peasants of overcrowded Java—a gesture to which, one supposes, Mao was not insensitive. All this, for short, was called 'Aiditism'.

Apart from its 3 million members, the PKI controlled 'mass organisations' with more than 13 million adherents. These included the communist-led Peasants' Front, Workers' Federation, Youth League and Women's Movement Association. In November 1963, the party gained representation for the first time in Sukarno's government; and in August 1964, one of Aidit's deputies, Njoto, was appointed to Sukarno's inner cabinet, thus achieving one of the PKI's major political objectives. In January 1965 came a further striking success, with the banning by the President of the PKI's main ideological rival, the Murba (Proletariat) party, which aimed at giving Indonesia a purely national form of communism, without international communist affiliations.

Aidit, however, aimed higher and farther still. As he put it in his May Day message for 1965, the working class must liberate the nation before liberating itself. The context helps one translate this communist jargon into plain English: 'The communists must rid the nation of all non-communist economic influence before taking over the government from the nationalists the communists now work with.' In the service of these aims, Aidit and his followers were working at two levels. From below, they were trying hard to infiltrate the armed forces, while their mobs spearheaded seizures of foreign enterprises, forcing the State to take them over. From above, they constantly criticised non-communist aspects of the government's economic policies, while continuing to praise Sukarno himself, thus manœuvring the President into adopting more and more of their programme.

For good measure, the PKI had taken to extending its subversive activities to the Philippines, much as an earlier generation of Indonesian communists did in the 1920s. In May 1965, an Indonesian student, Iljas Bakri, described as aged 39 (rather old, perhaps, for a student, but then he had been 'studying' at the University of the Philippines since 1958), and as a member of the PKI, was expelled from the Philippines for spying and trying to stir up anti-American feeling among fellow-students.

In July of the previous year, about thirty Indonesians rounded up for illegally entering the Philippines and stirring up trouble on Mindanao island had PKI membership cards. More 'trouble-makers'. (The Philippine Communist Party, illegal and in the doldrums, was showing fresh signs of militancy in mid-1965, with reports of renewed violence by their guerrilla and terrorist forces, known as the Huks.)

This astonishing run of good luck and success came to an abrupt end in the autumn of 1965, when the long-awaited showdown between the PKI and the Army, which had been expected *after* Sukarno's death or removal, took place while the President was still alive and in office. There is little doubt that the PKI had hoped to have far more time for its build-up against the Army. Traditionally, the higher officers of the Army had been anti-communist ever since they had crushed the 1948 communist uprising. But there had been some communist infiltration in the rank-and-file, and the junior officers were being brought up on a diet of NASAKOM, which blurred the distinction between the communists and the rest.

The communists had always had a foothold in the Indonesian Air Force, and early in March 1965 they seem to have tried —unsuccessfully—to spark off a mutiny in the Navy, spearheaded by a body called the 'Progressive and Revolutionary

Officers' Movement'. The police, too, had been a target for the PKI, and in April and May 1965, a number of higher-ranking officers, including the Commander of the Force, were dropped as a result of communist criticism of police attempts to control a mob which had attacked the Medan offices of the United States Information Service.

In the long term, however, the PKI had placed its hopes in a plan for a People's Militia of armed peasants under communist control. President Sukarno had resisted this plan but was beginning to lend an ear to an alternative plan for a 'Fifth Force' (i.e. in addition to the three Armed Services and the Police) of armed workers under communist direction. Ideally, one supposes, the PKI would have liked another two years or so for its plans to mature. A sudden deterioration in Sukarno's health, however, brought matters to a head. A Chinese physician who had been sent from Peking at the President's request to treat him for a kidney complaint, reported to the PKI that in his opinion his patient could not live much longer. The central committee of the Party called a secret emergency meeting at which plans for accelerated action were discussed.

At the first sign of the President's end, Stage One of the communist plan was to go into action. Leading generals and politicians were to be assassinated and a 'revolutionary' body—outwardly non-communist—was to take over. The communists' themselves were to come into the open in Stage Two, once all the anti-communists had been removed.

On September 29, Sukarno collapsed while addressing a meeting and the first stage started. Colonel Untung of the Palace Guard kidnapped Sukarno and sent murder squads into the homes of the leading Army generals, six of whom were horribly mutilated and murdered. A Revolutionary Council was proclaimed. The biggest of all PKI successes seemed at hand.

Yet the plot collapsed. The Army's Chief of Staff, General Jani, was among the murdered generals, but the murderers had botched the assassination of General Nasution, the Defence

Minister: his daughter was killed but he himself was only wounded. Moreover, a strongly anti-communist officer, General Suharto, stepped into Jani's shoes. Soon the Army was in *de facto* control, with the President ineffectually trying to pick up the shreds of his NASAKOM policy and angry mobs sacking PKI headquarters.

The Chinese, however, were 'in' the plot deeper than anybody had supposed. Armed PKI gangs began standing up to the Army, especially in central Java, and it turned out that their weapons had been shipped from China in large quantities. At the end of the year, the situation was confused, but the Army had the upper hand and the PKI's bluff had been called. Whatever the ultimate outcome of the struggle, the Party's long run of success had been halted.

* * *

In Malaysia and Singapore, the communists are incomparably weaker than in Indonesia. But they remain ingenious, persistent and, in the end, pretty formidable, though less so in Malaya proper (i.e. the Federation of Malaya, independent since 1957) than in Singapore and Sarawak: in Sabah (formerly North Borneo) the communists have had little success.

The parent body of Malayan communism is, in fact, the Chinese Communist Party; and the Malayan Communist Party (MCP), established in 1930, was at first a mere subsidiary of the Chinese party. By 1960, the four or five hundred hard-core remnants of the Malayan Communist Party's terrorist organisation had been driven across the Siamese border after twelve years of a murderous uprising, which started, as did the Indonesian communist rebellion and other similar outbreaks, in 1948 on Moscow's orders. The MCP, however, has retained its links with Peking and lately the New China News Agency and Peking Radio have been publishing its articles and statements. Terrorists whose camp on the Malayan-Siamese border was overrun by Malaysian security forces early in 1965 had been watching films made in Peking; which indicates a closer physical contact than had been thought likely.

Because the MCP is banned, it has been working underground and through various front organisations, the most active of which are the Socialist Front in Malaya and the Barisan Sosialis (which also means 'socialist front)' in Singapore. Both fronts are heavily infiltrated by communists; both have taken a vituperatively extreme anti-Malaysia line; but both recently split over the right degree of militancy to be adopted in opposing Malaysia. In December 1964, Dr Tan Chee-khoon, a leader of Malaya's Socialist Front, startled his more militant followers by declaring that the Front was against Indonesian aggression.

The issue then—Indonesian aggression—had, or appeared to have, patriotic overtones; and there was a similar note of patriotism about the issue that split the Barisan Sosialis in Singapore, in May 1964, when the Front's chairman, Dr Lee Siew-choh, resigned. Lee had called for an unqualified boycott of the call-up for military service, but a majority of other executive council members said the Front ought to support the government but 'under protest'.

Only the naive would suppose that this apparently more reasonable attitude implied, in the slightest degree, a change of heart. Patriotism was not, in fact, the real issue in either of the splits we have just discussed. What was at stake was simpler and more brutal: a question of tactics. Was a hard line or a soft line the more likely to bring the Socialist Front and the Barisan Sosialis to power? The Barisan Sosialis leaders who opposed an all-out boycott (the hard line) were not against a boycott as such; what they feared was a showdown that might cause the movement to suffer further heavy losses from arrests. Conversely, they argued, a hard line was wrong because 'the internal contradictions of the enemy' (i.e. the government) were not yet acute enough for a showdown to have the slightest chance of success. And the wave of arrests of hard line Socialist

Front men the following February seemed to prove Singapore's soft line men right.

Softness has never, on the other hand, been the line advocated by the militant Clandestine Communist Organisation (CCO) of Sarawak, and the aggressive posture of the Indonesian forces along the border has tended to prove *them* right, at least in their own eyes. There is a quaint official flavour about the expression 'Clandestine Communist Organisation', which must be explained. Clearly no Communist party would call itself a clandestine organisation, and the term was in fact coined by the Sarawak authorities to designate a number of communist-minded groups which never quite succeeded—because of official vigilance—in forming a proper Communist Party.

As in Malaya, an anti-Japanese resistance took root in Sarawak, and was dominated by local Chinese communists. It was known as the Sarawak Anti-Fascist League. Taking advantage of the wave of enthusiasm for communism which swept the Sarawak Chinese community after Mao Tse-tung's victory in China's civil war, remnants of the Anti-Fascist League formed the Sarawak Overseas Chinese Democratic League, a society dedicated to promoting Peking's policies through 'friendship' activities. The efficient Sarawak special branch, however, frustrated these activities, rendering the new League inoperative, so the communists tried again. This time their front was the Sarawak Advanced Youths' Association (SAYA), formed in 1956 and now the hard core of the CCO.

The CCO is a particularly interesting example of a fact which believers in normal democratic processes are often unwilling to grasp: that the size of a communist group bears little relation to its importance, that is, to its capacity to do damage. The Sarawak authorities believe that SAYA and the other often ephemeral groups that together constitute the CCO muster no more than 800 to 1,000 members between them. This is only 0·13 per cent of Sarawak's population of 770,000.

Yet despite this insignificant membership, the CCO's disruptive tactics have proved a tough problem for Sarawak and for Malaysia as a whole. True, its efforts to build up support among the peasants have come to very little, because the average Dayak in the rural areas has no fondness for the Chinese who form 100 per cent of the CCO's membership, and is suspicious of the Indonesians as well. But the CCO is well represented in the rudimentary trade union movement and gained considerable influence within the potentially powerful Sarawak United People's Party (SUPP).

Despite its sweeping title the SUPP is predominantly Chinese, and the fact that many of its members are prosperous businessmen has not inured them to communist persuasions. For three reasons, they are, in fact, receptive to CCO ideas: they want to cultivate trade relations with China; they believe China will come to dominate South-East Asia in time and want to insure themselves for the future; and they oppose Malaysia because they fear that it may lead to the imposition of anti-Chinese measures by Tunku Abdul Rahman's Malay-dominated administration in Kuala Lumpur, the federal capital. Paradoxically, this fear has led the SUPP to lend itself to subversion which benefits not only the COC but also Indonesia, which treats its Chinese community far more harshly than Malaysia does.*

Between them, the CCO and the SUPP have provided about 1,000 trainees for the guerrilla warfare camps set up by the Indonesian army in the jungles across the border. The first batch of trainees went to Indonesia in 1963, and since then many of them have returned for fleeting, murderous—and largely unsuccessful—raids into Sarawak. In the early stages of the 'confrontation', the raiding parties received much help from a SUPP branch at Lundu, in eastern Sarawak, but the Sarawak government closed the branch down in May 1964. The Indonesians and their local Chinese communist allies had

* Splits between moderates and extremists have blurred the picture, however, since these lines were written.

hoped to set up a 'liberated area' in this part of Sarawak, but lacked the most essential ingredient of success for guerrilla fighters: popular support.

The CCO, and of course the Malayan and Singaporean fronts mentioned earlier, have forged links with Indonesia's PKI. Indeed Djakarta, Indonesia's capital, teams with Malayan exile fronts or groups, all more or less under communist control. The ramifications of subversion are thus multilateral. The PKI works inwards in Indonesia, and outwards in Malaysia and the Philippines. The Chinese Communist Party, for its part, has no need to intervene directly in Malaysia, for it is already well served by the Malayan Communist Party, Sarawak's CCO and the front organisations. The trouble-makers' league is, in fact, an international.

4
The Take-over Bidders

═══════

THE SPLITS in various Communist parties in East Asia are all relevant to a study of the struggle for the Third World, since these reflect the ceaseless fight between Russians and Chinese to gain or retain control over individual parties, with the same long-term aim of controlling the country in which each party operates. Space limitations, however, rule out detailed treatment of all cases, interesting though each case is in its own rights. A few words about recent developments in India, Japan, Ceylon, Burma and Siam, may lend some perspective—although necessarily incomplete—to the struggle in the Far East.

In each of the countries I have just named, the Communist Party is in opposition, not in power. Only three Asian Communist parties, apart from China's, are actually in power, and Mongolia sided with Moscow, and North Vietnam and North Korea with Peking, at least until Soviet military help for North Vietnam caused some heart-searching both in North Korea and in North Vietnam. When in opposition, however, Communist parties have less natural sense of identity and are more exposed to conflicting pulls and pressures.

In India, for instance, the Communist Party has split down the middle, not so much on the Sino-Soviet issue as on the Sino-Indian contention. There are now two Communist parties in India. The Moscow-oriented party consists of communists who took a 'patriotic', anti-Chinese line during China's invasion of contested Himalayan territory in 1962. A Peking-oriented party, consisting of those who support China's case against India (and against Moscow) was formed in November 1964.

The 'Peking' party is, of course, the more militant of the two.

It claims 60 per cent of the old United Party's membership, but some 900 of its senior members were arrested at the end of 1964, allegedly for plotting an armed rebellion. This did not, however, prevent the 'Peking' party from winning forty seats in the Kerala State elections in March 1965, compared with three 'Moscow' victories, even though many of the winning 'Peking' candidates were behind bars.

In Japan, a crisis developed on the issue of the partial nuclear test ban treaty. Two of the Communist Party's nine parliamentary representatives were expelled from the party in May 1964 for having supported ratification of the treaty. With other anti-Peking expellees, they have since set up a small Moscow-oriented group.

In Ceylon, the pro-Peking faction of the Communist Party found its own organisation in January 1964 and attacked the pro-Moscow 'revisionists' for having joined two other Marxist groups (including the Trotskyists) in a United Left Front which was ready to use parliamentary methods to reach power.

In Burma, General Ne Win, head of the Revolutionary Junta, had some 700 mainly Moscow-line communists arrested in November 1963 following the breakdown of the government's talks with the guerrillas of the Burma Communist Party. The guerrillas themselves were pro-Peking and their leaders had flown to Rangoon from Peking for the talks; but Ne Win was taking no chances; and rightly, for while the guerrillas were spreading destruction in the countryside, the Moscow-line men, members of the so-called National United Front, were trying to gain control of the administration from within. Though the guerrillas never look like winning—unless the Chinese start helping them in earnest—they are still fighting on, eighteen years after they first took up arms against the first independent Burma government in 1948.

There is no discernible Moscow influence among the communists in Burma's neighbour, Siam (Thailand). The small and illegal Communist Party of Thailand, whose members are mostly Thais of Chinese origin, takes its orders from Peking.

Strictly internal subversion has been kept to a minimum by a succession of anti-communist governments which brought Siam into the South-East Asia Collective Defence Treaty (SEATO) in 1954 and kept it in. But Siam now faces a new threat of concerted subversion from China, Laos and North Vietnam.

Early in 1965, communist radio stations in these three countries announced the formation of two new 'fronts', called the 'Thailand Independence Movement' and the 'Patriotic Front of Thailand' and commented with approval on the plans of these bodies to overthrow the Siamese government. Simultaneously, there was a sudden increase in communist subversion in Siam's north-eastern provinces, which adjoin Laos and whose population is mostly ethnically akin to the Laotians. Agents from the communist-led Pathet Lao movement—itself controlled from North Vietnam—were crossing the Mekong river to stir up separatist feelings among the local people. This kind of thing had been occurring, on and off, for years, but the sudden increase in infiltration, coupled with the launching of the two bodies I have named (which were fused in December 1965), suggested that Siam was likely to find itself under intensified pressure.

* * *

Of greater dramatic interest, perhaps, are the rival attempts by the Soviet Union and China to exploit the troubled situations we have examined in the last two chapters. It will be seen that the Sino-Soviet split has not removed the external communist threat that weighs on Indochina and Indonesia, but merely complicated it.

In Stalin's day, the Soviet Communist Party's grip on the Indochina and Indonesian parties was firm; though for geographical and historical reasons, the Chinese party had a job to do, especially in Indochina. In those days, however, the Chinese party, though doubtless always a difficult and outspoken partner in private councils, was invariably loyal to Moscow in public utterances.

There was thus no special problem, from Moscow's viewpoint, in the bilateral relations between the Chinese party and other Asian parties, or in any unilateral action the Chinese might take. It was on Moscow's orders that the Communist parties of India, Burma, Indonesia and the Philippines launched insurrections in 1948; but China approved, helped to train Philippine guerrillas and kept in touch with the Malayan terrorists.

Stalin, on the other hand, approved (for he had nothing to lose) when Mao threw his People's Volunteers into the Korean War. And in the Indochina war, cooperation seems to have been reasonably harmonious: Soviet and Czech arms of all sorts reached the Vietminh forces by land across China, together with more direct help from the Chinese themselves.

This picture of fraternal harmony in disruption has been shattered by Khrushchev's 'revisionism' and by Mao's unwillingness to follow either him or his successors on the path of rapprochement with the United States in the interests of freedom from nuclear war (though not, remember, from all wars, for as we have seen, this was never Khrushchev's idea).

In practice, however, as distinct from theory and public statements, Peking has been consistently wary, since the Korean war, of venturing into situations that might lead China into a major war with the United States. True, there was a danger of 'Hiroshima-type' atomic war during China's intervention in Korea; but the incomparably more destructive thermo-nuclear bomb had not been tested at that time. Just such a situation might have arisen from, say, an attempt by the North Vietnamese Army to invade South Vietnam across the no-man's-land along the 17th parallel, which had been drawn by the international negotiators at Geneva in 1954, when the first Indochina war was brought to an end.

The danger of a direct North Vietnamese aggression of this type was at its most acute from July 1955, when the Diem government in South Vietnam turned down the suggestion made in the unsigned Final Declaration of the Geneva conference for electoral consultations between North and South Vietnam. There is evidence that the victorious Commander-in-Chief of the North Vietnamese Army, General Vo Nguyen Giap, was strongly in favour of invading South Vietnam, calculating that the rewards of victory would be swift and that the Great Powers, including America, would be faced with an irreversible accomplished fact. At that time, however, the international movement was still disciplined and monolithic; Moscow still gave the orders and the Lao Dong party, among others, obeyed. Not long before, the Soviet Communist Party had laid down a new general line for the reunification of divided countries, the gist of which was that this was a matter to be decided between the governments of both sections of the country.

Now in taking this line the Russians were thinking primarily of avoiding the embarrassing possibility of free elections throughout Germany, in which the weak and unpopular East German communist regime would have been swamped. But this was now to be the general line for the world communist movement, and it frustrated North Vietnam of its design for aggression against the South. It is known that angry clashes on this issue took place within the Lao Dong party.

In September 1955, however, the North Vietnamese party accepted a local variant of the general communist line, when it set up the Fatherland Front with the object of unifying Vietnam through consultations between 'various political parties, armies, mass organisations, circles and personalities of the two zones' of the country; leading to general elections. This was a clear attempt to by-pass the Diem government in the South, by threatening, in effect, to set up bodies that would 'consult' with the North and 'agree' on electoral arrangements to Hanoi's taste that would appear to satisfy the requirements of the Geneva conference.

At that time, there was little chance of achieving this policy, for Diem had established complete control over South Vietnam. The chance came rather more than two years later when the private armies of the politico-religious sects, which Diem had defeated, took up arms against him. Communist guerrillas in South Vietnam who had hidden their arms when France was defeated, dug them up again, joined the insurgents and soon controlled the insurrection. By 1959, when the insurrection had become a serious threat to the Diem regime, Moscow's authority over the world communist movement had already weakened. The Lao Dong party was far from happy about this, as it preferred to take orders from distant Russia rather than from China, which was uncomfortably close.

But Ho Chi Minh and Giap may well have thought that the incipient division in the communist movement could be exploited for North Vietnamese ends. At any rate in May 1959, the party took the fateful decision to 'liberate' South Vietnam by force. Neither China nor Russia, however, was in favour of direct aggression, and it so happened that the insurrectionary situation in the South made it possible to avoid sending the North Vietnamese Army openly across the dividing line. The method chosen, therefore, was indirect aggression by means of a 'people's war'. This, it was reckoned, would neither invite international disapproval nor risk the generalised nuclear war which neither Moscow nor Peking wanted.

There are some indications that the Russians have nevertheless tried, from time to time, to restrain the North Vietnamese, particularly in Laos, where their activities were embarrassing to the Soviet government. But as the Sino-Soviet rift widened, and as the insurrection in South Vietnam escalated into war, Moscow gradually lost influence over Hanoi.

The final turning point came in the summer of 1963, when Russia called on the North Vietnamese to sign the three-power partial nuclear test ban treaty and China told them not to. China was closer. The North Vietnamese denounced the treaty and thereby sided with Peking in the Sino-Soviet dispute. This was certainly not what Ho Chi Minh would have liked, as it was to North Vietnam's interest to play off Moscow against Peking and this was no longer possible once Ho had come off the fence on which he had been skilfully balancing for many years. The upshot of his decision, however, was that Moscow lost its last shreds of control over the North Vietnamese Communists.

Now the Soviet government and party have no taste for situations which they can't control. Even before Hanoi's refusal to endorse the test ban treaty, they had decided that Laos was such a situation. At the end of 1960, the Russians had started airlifting arms to General (then captain) Kong Lae, a neutralist who had joined forces with the communists to fight the American-backed right-wingers. By 1963, Kong Lae had become disillusioned with the communists and was using Soviet planes to bomb their forces. This was too much for the Russians, and they withdrew their planes—and the technicians they had also sent the neutralists—in the spring of that year.

At this stage, Khrushchev had still not decided that Indochina as a whole was more trouble than it was worth. He didn't want a major involvement that might lead to another dangerous confrontation with America—one Cuba 1962 was enough; but on the other hand, he was embarrassed by Peking's ever shriller denunciations of his 'revisionism'. His way out was to reaffirm Soviet support for 'national liberation' wars, while limiting actual military commitments as far as possible.

On December 6, 1963, for instance, *Pravda* claimed that neither the national liberation movement nor the class struggle against capitalism was affected by peaceful co-existence. The Soviet Communist Party's duty was to give all political and economic support—'and, if necessary, support by arms'. Khrushchev himself, in his speech before the Egyptian National Assembly in Cairo on May 11, 1964, argued that there was no contradiction between giving weapons to nationalists struggling against 'imperialism', and a policy of peaceful co-existence with the West.

Khrushchev, in other words, still felt the need to compete with Mao in support for 'national liberation' movements, the control of which might otherwise pass by default to the Chinese. This interpretation squares with what went on at a little-noticed trade union conference held in Hanoi between October 20 and 23, 1963. One relevant point is that it was sponsored by the Soviet-dominated World Federation of Trade Unions, one of the biggest communist international front organisations, whose headquarters are in Prague. Another point was that China as well as Russia was represented at the meeting, although by that time Khrushchev and Mao were on shouting terms only. An 'international solidarity committee' was set up with the avowed objects of calling on the workers of the world to agitate for the withdrawal of the American forces in South Vietnam, and to get various countries to recognise the Hanoi-controlled National Front for the Liberation of South Vietnam. The concealed aims of the Russians in calling this conference can perhaps be guessed. One was certainly to demonstrate to other communists that the Russians, no matter what the Chinese might say to them, were as strongly committed to supporting the national liberation movement as the Chinese themselves. Another hidden aim was presumably to create an ostensibly non-political workers' body through which to channel funds and material to the Vietcong guerrillas in South Vietnam. Some months later, on March 16, 1964, Hanoi radio reported that the Soviet trade unions were to made a gift of 100,000 roubles' worth of medical supplies to the NFLSV.

Now the 100,000 roubles (less than £9,000 at the official rate of exchange) mentioned by Hanoi radio is scarcely a large enough sum to conceal deliveries of military material. There was indeed no evidence at that time that Russia had sent military supplies to South Vietnam, and in January 1964 the Hanoi press started accusing the Russians of diverting the South Vietnamese from armed revolution, and thus abetting the Americans. Whatever the justification for this complaint, the Soviet Tass Agency felt the need, on February 25, to announce approval of the National Liberation Front's policies, adding that the Soviet Union would give assistance to the national liberation struggle in South Vietnam.

By the summer of 1964, Khrushchev seems, however, to have decided that he wanted no more part of Indochina's continuing crisis. On July 26, 1964, the Soviet government threatened to withdraw from the 'co-chairmanship' of the Geneva conference, which it had shared with Britain and under which both governments tacitly agreed to sort out difficulties arising out of the Geneva agreements. This threat was made on the eve of a visit to Moscow of Mr R. A. Butler (as he was), the then British Foreign Secretary. Mr Butler is said to have formed the impression, from an outspoken private talk with the ebullient Khrushchev, that the Soviet leader realised Russia's influence had waned and had no taste for further embroilments in Indochina.

At this stage, it could be deduced that the Soviet Communist Party, caught on the horns of its insoluble dilemma—whether to seek an understanding with America or help America's enemies in the interests of world communism—had opted for the former. A truer interpretation would be that he wanted to avoid both the danger of a confrontation with the US, in Laos or Vietnam, *and* the odium of appearing to support American 'imperialism' in Indochina.

There was no such easy way out, however. Khrushchev's colleagues on the all-powerful party Presidium revolted against his apparent willingness to lose control over the world communist movement for the sake of an understanding with America. On October 16, 1964, less than three months after his meeting with Mr Butler, Khrushchev was overthrown.

Those who thought the younger men who took over from Khrushchev would prove softer and less revolutionary than he had been were soon disappointed. As we saw earlier, it was after Khrushchev's fall that the Soviet Union started helping Algeria and the UAR to airlift supplies to the Congolese rebels. And it was the new men who reversed his decision to wash his hands of Indochina. The first sign of this came in December

1964, when the Russians invited the National Front for the Liberation of South Vietnam to set up a permanent office in Moscow. Now the extraordinary thing was that this hadn't happened long before. The NFLSF already had offices in Peking, Algiers, Djakarta, Prague, East Berlin and Havana. But not in Moscow—a clear sign of strained relations between the Soviet and North Vietnamese Communist parties.

Competitive involvement was at work. The Vietcong guerrillas seemed to be doing well in South Vietnam and there was, at that time, no sign that the United States might be preparing to step up its military aid to the South Vietnamese government. Looking ahead, the Russians doubtless foresaw that some time or other there would have to be an internationally negotiated settlement in Vietnam. If they divorced themselves completely from the conflict this would leave the Chinese with a dominant communist voice at the peace table. This was a strong consideration, but there was an even more powerful and pressing one.

The Soviet Communist Party was desperately trying to attract the world's Communist parties to Moscow for a conference at which the Chinese would have been made either to toe the Moscow line or be read out of the international communist movement. The Chinese, naturally, were refusing to go, and the East Asian parties, including the Lao Dong party, were supporting them by threatening to boycott the conference, too. To Khrushchev's successors, these circumstances seemed to offer a golden opportunity to win the North Vietnamese party back to the Moscow fold. They had—or thought they had—an unbeatable trump in that they were in a position to offer North Vietnam up-to-date military equipment, whereas the Chinese were not. Would this not be the way to bring the North Vietnamese Communists back into line and perhaps start a landslide in Moscow's favour?

This seems to have been the reasoning behind a Tass statement on November 26, 1964, pledging all necessary help to North Vietnam. And it was hardly surprising that a powerful

Soviet delegation, headed by the new Soviet Premier, Kosygin, left for Hanoi early in February 1965, or that the delegation included Air Marshal Vershinin, Russia's vice-Minister of Defence, and Mr Loginov, the minister of Civil Aviation. It was assumed that Vershinin would be discussing defence arrangements and Loginov arranging for air transport of arms (or even men) to North Vietnam.

The North Vietnamese, however, spoilt it all by overplaying their hand. Probably in the hope of provoking the Russians into giving all-out pledge of military aid against the United States, they ordered their southern guerrillas into action. On February 7, a day after Kosygin's arrival in Hanoi, the Vietcong made their first direct attacks on American military installations in South Vietnam, killing or wounding seventy Americans and destroying seventeen helicopters and three transport planes. A few hours later, American jet fighters launched a series of bombing attacks on North Vietnam. This was escalation and it was more than Kosygin had bargained for; indeed he is believed to have been both surprised and indignant at the Vietcong's attack.

Embarrassed, too. On February 7, just before the news of the American bombing, Kosygin, in a speech in Hanoi, had repeated Russia's pledge to help North Vietnam, but *Pravda* on February 8, while mentioning that he had made a speech, didn't report what he had said. Next day, *Pravda* merely warned the United States that any more bombing might prejudice the improvement of Soviet-American relations. This was hardly a threat; and hardly enough to make the North Vietnamese disown Peking. Indeed Kosygin's visit to Hanoi seems to have flopped. There was no sign that the Russians had made firm offers of equipment. Nor did they win any ideological concessions from the North Vietnamese. And when the time came, on March 1, the Lao Dong party duly boycotted the Moscow conference, as the Chinese had told them they must.

Since then, the Russians have continued to be torn between

their desire to avoid a clash with the Americans and their desire to demonstrate to the communist world that they alone are willing and able to help North Vietnam in its plight. The Chinese have not made things easy for them. They themselves have no more liking for a dangerous involvement than the Russians have. In February 1965, Mao Tse-tung told the well-known American correspondent, Edgar Snow, that the Vietnamese 'people' could win their war unaided and that China would not fight unless its own territory was attacked. But this didn't prevent the Chinese press from keeping up a continuous barrage of taunts at the Russians for failing to do enough to support North Vietnam, or alternatively, for giving aid merely for the purpose of striking a bargain with America at Hanoi's expense.

In the face of such taunts, the Russians have refrained from all-out assistance to Hanoi, but have not altogether resisted the temptations of competitive involvement. May brought reports that the Russians had constructed anti-aircraft missile sites in North Vietnam and a warning from Mr Dean Rusk, the American Secretary of State, against going too far.

Indonesia

For Russia, Indonesia must be a tantalising problem: at once a temptation and an embarrassment. With its rich resources and strategic situation, the Indonesian islands would be a dramatic gain for communism, and the West would suffer if deprived of their raw materials, should this be one outcome of a communist take-over. On the other hand, Russia and the European communist bloc could scarcely provide alternative markets for Indonesia's rubber, tin, sugar and oil. It is bad enough having to buy Cuba's sugar. Again, it would be a great success for Soviet policy to be able to keep Indonesia out of China's grip. But the PKI, which had grown strong on Moscow's 'constitutional' recipe for success, rewarded the Russians by siding with Peking in the Sino-Soviet ideological dispute.

Doubtless these thoughts have often crossed the minds of

Khrushchev and his successors. There have indeed been many signs of special Soviet interest in Indonesia. Since 1961, the Russians have sold arms worth at least £350 million to President Sukarno's government. The Indonesian State being permanently near bankruptcy, these huge sales would not have been possible without Soviet credits; and without them, Sukarno's confrontation with Malaysia would hardly, in turn, have been possible.

The Russians and their friends have lost no chances of saying or doing things that would please Sukarno. For instance, the Soviet Union and Czechoslovakia were the only two members of the United Nations Security Council to support Indonesia against Malaysia's complaint of aggression in September 1964. And when Sukarno visited Moscow in 1964, the communiqué, issued on October 1, recorded Soviet support for 'the liberation struggle of the peoples of North Kalimantan'—a reference to the fiction that Indonesia is helping the peoples of Sabah, Sarawak and Brunei to free themselves from British imperialism and 'neo-colonialism'.

There are strong grounds for believing that in 1962 and 1963, the Russians seriously toyed with the idea of trying to stage a Cuba-type take-over in Indonesia. In July 1962, Mr Mikoyan, then Khrushchev's principal trouble-shooter, went to Djakarta, ostensibly to attend the Asian Games, but in reality because the Indonesian war of nerves against Dutch New Guinea, then entering its last phase, seemed to offer interesting possibilities of exploitation. He is believed to have proposed that negotiations with the Dutch should be broken off and a full-scale invasion of West New Guinea launched; and that the PKI should be given half a dozen seats in the Cabinet. In return, the Russians would have been prepared to offer the £130 million worth of arms the Indonesians had purchased up to then, as a free gift, plus unlimited credits for economic purchases. One must presume the offer misfired, for Mikoyan, who had arrived on July 20 planning to stay eight days, left precipitately on the 24th.

The Soviet Defence Minister, Marshal Malinovsky, may well have put similar proposals, substituting Borneo for New Guinea, on a visit he made to Djakarta in April 1963. But Malinovsky evidently hoped to do something about the wayward Indonesian communists, for he spent an hour with the PKI's leader, Aidit, shortly after his arrival. Malinovsky doesn't seem to have achieved very much, but the Chinese were apparently worried lest he might have, for they sent President Liu Shao-ch'i to Indonesia almost as soon as he had left. In June 1964, Mr Mikoyan made a second trip to Djakarta, but this time, as far as I know, his main concern was to get the Indonesians to start paying Russia back for the arms they had 'bought'. Repayments were, in fact, to begin in 1965, but Mikoyan soon found out that the Indonesians had reason on their side in asking for a deferment: after all, they had no money. And he decided Soviet deliveries should continue anyway.

It is not difficult to guess the motives of Soviet leaders in their Indonesian policy. Although the Russians wanted the PKI in the cabinet in 1962, they must long since have realised that though this aim has since been fulfilled, they had gained nothing from the PKI's success. One must assume, indeed, that the Russians are not particularly interested in seeing Indonesia come under the rule of a Communist Party that is, for all practical purposes, in alliance with Peking. The Russians moreover must have known that the Indonesian Army was the only body that might conceivably challenge and defeat an attempt by the PKI to seize power after Sukarno's death or retirement. And they were aware that the arms Moscow had provided strengthened the Army.

Another consideration, from Moscow's standpoint, has been that Russia's attempts to strengthen its foothold in the Afro-Asian movement had been frustrated by the Chinese and Indonesian Communist parties, working in concert. As we saw in the first chapter of this book this Sino-Indonesian combination was successful in keeping the Russians out of the new

Afro-Asian Journalists' association. And later on the two Asian parties opposed Russia's claim to be invited to the 'second Bandung' conference (which was to open in Algiers in June 1965, but was postponed because of the overthrow of the Algerian President, Ben Bella).

These things, in combination, explain why the Russians have concentrated on building up good relations with the Indonesian *State* rather than with the PKI. In providing aid and support for the Sukarno Government, they may have hoped both to make Indonesia dependent on Russia and to persuade Sukarno and his ministers to plead Moscow's case in the Third World. It is hardly surprising to know that within Indonesia itself the Russians had taken to supporting not the PKI but the Murba (Proletarian) Party which the PKI considered to be its principal rival as a nationalist Marxist grouping. It was thus a blow to Russia when Sukarno, yielding before PKI pressure, banned the Murba party in January 1965 (as we saw in the last chapter).

While this situation lasted, Peking was, quite simply, sitting pretty. The PKI supported them against the Soviet Communist Party, and Sukarno was fighting China's 'imperialist' enemies. In Malaysia itself, subversion was safely in the hands of the overwhelmingly Chinese Malayan Communist Party and its front organisations in Singapore and Sarawak. There was therefore no need for the Chinese to intervene directly in the Malaysian crisis, or to spend vast sums in Indonesia. When the Indonesian Foreign Minister, Dr Subandrio, visited Peking in January 1965, to find out, as he said, how much military aid China would give Indonesia if Britain attacked, he soon learned the limitations of China's reticence. He returned, in fact, with a communiqué recording China's support, a vague agreement to 'strengthen friendly contacts in the military field' and credit cover for £35 million of Indonesian purchases.

When Sukarno himself, on May 25, announced that 'the guiding line of the struggle of Indonesia and the Chinese People's Republic is identical', Mao Tse-tung must have thought that such friendship was cheap at the price. And Kosygin, who went on sending arms to Indonesia, must have reflected that he wasn't getting much for his money.

IV

The Latin
American Magnet

I

A Special Case

COMMUNISM in Latin America is not the same as communism anywhere else in the world. For one thing, it has always been more anarchically untidy than anywhere else. There have been disciplined Moscow-line parties, more or less Trotskyist groups and a whole spectrum of revolutionary Socialist parties, often well to the left of orthodox Communist parties in their un-bridled advocacy of violence. The advent of Fidelismo and Peking's attempts to win over Latin American Communists have merely added complexity to an already exceedingly complicated picture.

One thing is clear, however: all these groupings or parties of the extreme Left, whether they listen to Moscow or Peking or Havana, or go their own way to perdition, are dedicated to overthrowing the existing order. Since many Latin American regimes are still oligarchic despotisms of one kind or another, the soil is extraordinarily fertile for harvests of revolutionary success. Moreover, the tenacity of anti-Yanqui sentiments throughout Latin America has played into the hands of extremists of the Left even more than of the Right, so that many Latin Americans, especially among the intellectuals, have fallen, some more some less unconsciously, for the syllogism: we are anti-Yanqui and the Yanquis are anti-communist and anti-socialist; therefore we are pro-communist and pro-socialist. Indeed if fragmentation were not a general law of politics in Latin America, communism would doubtless have made more headway than in fact it has.

It all began conventionally enough with the creation of Latin American Communist parties in the 1920s, at a time when the Bolshevik faith in world revolution did not seem an improbable proposition. In retrospect, it can be seen that the Brazilian communists, in particular, have tried everything in their sustained bid for power. There was an abortive revolt in 1924 and a failed *coup d'état* in 1935, with years of sporadic guerrilla warfare in between; and in the 1960s, a nearly successful attempt to subvert the State from within. The leading figure in all these events was the veteran communist leader, Luiz Carlos Prestes, who was not, however, a communist in a formal sense when he led the so-called National Liberation Alliance (a 'front' controlled by the Communist Party) into revolt in 1924 or when he headed the peasant guerrillas of his 'Prestes column' until their dispersal in 1927.

During the long exile that followed, Prestes spent four years in Moscow, studying revolutionary tactics and Marxism-Leninism. It was only in 1935, when he returned to Brazil, that Prestes joined the Brazilian Communist Party. Ten years later, just after the Second World War (in which Brazil fought on the side of the allies, including Russia), the party polled 600,000 votes, returning Prestes himself to the Senate and eight other communists to the Chamber of Deputies. This was the high water mark of Brazilian communism. In 1947, the party was banned and support for it plummeted.

Communists are not, however, deterred by manifest lack of popular support: power, not popularity, is what they are interested in, and power can be won in many ways. And early in 1964, Prestes and his party came uncomfortably close to taking over from the complacent hands of a vain and ineffectual Head of State, President João Goulart, himself a wealthy landowner who sought personal popularity by a vaguely reformist programme, thought he could use the communists to serve his own ends, and placed many communists or near-communists in influential positions. The bloodless and popular *coup d'état* of Marshal Castello Branco at the end of March 1964 removed Goulart and with him the immediate communist threat.

I have started with Brazil, and I shall come back to Brazil.

This is logical, for Brazil is at once the United States, the Soviet Union and the China of Latin America—vast and populous, its booming industries a triumph of state-aided private enterprise, its peasant masses a temptation to Maoist or Fidelist theoreticians of guerrilla war, its intellectuals receptive to Marxist persuasions and its proletariat a field for Soviet ploughing. If Brazil became a communist State, no other Latin American country would be safe; the United States would be outflanked and the strategic picture of the Western hemisphere would be transformed. The danger of world war might, indeed, become acute. After all, the installation of Soviet rockets in Cuba, a small island in the Caribbean, brought the world to the brink of a nuclear explosion in 1962. But Cuba, as Americans might put it, is 'peanuts', in comparison with Brazil.

Such considerations help to explain the Soviet dilemma in Latin America. On the one hand, control of Latin America would, at least in theory, isolate the United States which, in communist parlance, is still the 'main enemy' as the citadel of world 'capitalism'. On the other hand, the advent of nuclear weapons has made any major communist victory in Latin America prohibitively dangerous. The Monroe Doctrine and the post-war history of American interventions in the area, from Guatemala in 1954 to the Dominican Republic in 1965, suggests that the United States would not allow another and bigger communist take-over. (True, Cuba did 'go communist', but this was due to special circumstances, which we shall examine later.)

There is, moreover, an economic angle to the Soviet dilemma. Fidel Castro's victory in Cuba, which was violently anti-American from the start, deprived that island of its privileged sugar market in the United States. The Russians found themselves having to provide an alternative market, and indeed to underwrite the whole Cuban economy. This soon proved an enormous burden which, according to some estimates, was running at the rate of nearly £700 million a year in 1964. This is a huge sum for an already overburdened economy to find—enough to make the Russians wonder whether they could afford a communist victory in one of the more important Latin American countries. Could the Soviet Union, for instance, provide a market for Brazil's coffee, or even for Chile's copper?

Victory, then, is expensive as well as dangerous. Yet ideology dictates continuing interference, even if State policy sometimes applies the brakes. This, as we have seen in earlier chapters, is the great and unresolved dilemma of Soviet policy in its present phase. It is a particularly acute one in Latin America, for the glittering (though hypothetical) prize of 'final victory' over capitalism acts like a magnet while the dangers and financial disadvantages act as a repellent.

The events of 1956—Khrushchev's denunciation of Stalin at the Twentieth Congress of the Soviet Communist Party and the revolutions in Poland and Hungary—shook the Latin American parties no less than others. A tremendous effort to revive them was launched by the Russians on the occasion of the fortieth anniversary of the Bolshevik Revolution in November 1957, when the leaders of sixty-six Communist parties met in Moscow. During the conference, the leaders of the Latin American parties received new orders from the Soviet party. Communists throughout the area were called upon to support or set up 'popular front' alliances with any appropriate groups that would collaborate with them, whether Labour, Socialist or Nationalist. It is not by coincidence that immediately after the 1957 conference Luiz Carlos Prestes publicly renounced the principle of revolutionary violence and called upon the Brazilian party to seek a 'parliamentary road to socialism' (that is, to communism).

The Russians were pleased with the Brazilian and Chilean communists, and said so: in November 1958—a year after the Moscow meeting—a leading Soviet figure, Boris N. Ponomarev, singled out Brazil and Chile as two countries in which 'national front movements' exemplified the 'kind of cooperation the Soviet party would like to see between communist and trade union and political movements in capitalist countries'. Chile, indeed, has a remarkably obedient and well disciplined party—doubtless the best in Latin America from Moscow's point of view.

Though of scruffy appearance and uncharismatic personality, the Chilean party leader, Luis Corvalán, had succeeded in establishing an electoral coalition with the Socialists and other left-wing groups. This alliance, known as FRAP (or Popular Revolutionary Action Front), grew into a formidable force but was decisively defeated by Eduardo Frei (now President of Chile) and his Christian Democrats in the Presidential and Congressional elections of September 1964 and March 1965, respectively.

As the new communist line unfolded in 1958, a new emphasis on links and dealings with Latin America was evident in the communist capitals. Communist radio stations and newspapers stepped up their coverage of Latin American affairs. Trade and cultural missions were sent out and Latin Americans in ever larger numbers were invited to Peking and Moscow, which were still united, at least in public, in a brotherhood of disruption. The Czechs sent film stars to a festival in Santiago de Chile. In October 1958, Khrushchev granted an interview to a Brazilian correspondent, in which he drew a contrast between Soviet 'non-interference' and United States 'aggression' in Latin America. The international communist fronts—especially the World Federation of Trade Unions, the International Union of Students and the World Peace Council—redoubled their efforts to entice Latin American individuals and groups to participate in their gatherings. In August—still in 1958—the New China News Agency published interviews with 'peace' delegates from Argentina, Brazil, Chile, Colombia, Cuba and Paraguay, who were on a visit to Peking. A few days later, Chou En-lai himself told the delegates about Latin America's role in furtherance of anti-imperialism. Euphoria reigned in a glow of Sino-Soviet anti-Yanquism.

Fidelismo and the acrimonies of the Sino-Soviet dispute changed all that. In January 1959, Fidel Castro made his triumphal entry into Havana. Though not, at that time, a communist in any formal sense, he had communists among his entourage: the Argentine-born guerrilla warfare specialist, Ernesto 'Che' Guevara, for instance. Under his rule, Cuba's relations with the United States were soon at their worst and he was turning to Russia for help.

This was encouraging from Moscow's point of view, but the Soviet theoreticians were still bothered. The 'official' Cuban Communist Party had played little part in Castro's insurrection and the Soviet theoreticians mistrusted revolutionaries, however anti-American and anti-capitalist, who stayed aloof from the communists. The situation, however, was too promising to be ignored, so (not for the first time or the last) theory was adjusted to meet reality and consecrate hopes. The outcome was the 'creation' of a new category of States, to be known as 'national democracies'—a designation tailor-made to fit the Cuban case. As we have seen in earlier chapters, this idea was launched at the end of 1960 in the World Communist Declaration issued in Moscow after the conference of eighty-one Communist parties, in which Russia and the rest pledged help to the 'national liberation movement'. This was the last time the Chinese and the Russians, albeit with visible difficulty, managed to agree on the final draft of a text and jointly sign it. From then on, the rift between Moscow and Peking grew too wide for concealment.

From then on, also, two new factors transformed the communist scene in Latin America. One was Cuban subversion; the other was an anti-Soviet drive by Chinese agents, initially small in scale, but persistent, perhaps to the point of permanence. We shall be looking at Cuba's activities in fuller detail in the next section. The point to be made here is that the Russians, whatever reservations they may have had about peasant insurrections, were drawn more and more into supporting Fidel Castro's efforts to subvert the independent countries of continental Latin America by armed violence. This, once more, was competitive subversion. In the 1920s, Prestes had tried guerrilla warfare in Brazil and failed. In 1957, the Russians had told Latin American communists to seek power by infiltration and other 'legal' methods. No matter: the Cubans were now supporting bandit and guerrilla movements and the Chinese were going round saying the Russians were soft, bourgeois and revisionist.

The Russians could not, in these circumstances, afford to appear less revolutionary than the Cubans or Chinese. True, if there were any substance in Khrushchev's boast of non-interference, the Russians would stay aloof—virtuous in their correctness. Latin America, after all, is hardly a vital, or even a major, State interest of the Soviet Union; and the Russians would not actually *suffer* if they refrained from aiding and abetting subversion there (or indeed elsewhere).

But communism as a *faith*, however fragmented it might seem as a *movement*, is a proselytising force, and the Russians are still the highest of its high priests. To refrain from supporting subversion when others are at it could cost them the allegiance of Latin America's Communist parties. Genuine non-interference would not hurt the Soviet peoples or damage their State interests; but loss of the faithful would be intolerable to the Soviet Communist Party.

The Chinese, in fact, had soon shown how the faithful could be subverted and enticed. As early as 1961 a thousand of the 30,000 or so Brazilian Communists had pooled their indignation against the 'revisionists' (Krushchev's faithful in the Brazilian Communist Party) and formed a party of their own, the Communist Party of Brazil. Soon the Communist Party of Brazil was passing pro-Chinese resolutions.

Now one might well ask: What do a thousand pro-Peking Brazilian Communists matter? But Soviet communists do not look at numbers in the same way as parliamentary democrats used to counting 'Ayes' and 'Noes' of equal worth. They know the value of a hard revolutionary core and appreciate the menace of a dissident nucleus. Besides, the Chinese have since shown, as the Russians rightly feared they would, that their success in Brazil was not a flash in the pan, for pro-Peking groups have sprung up in Bolivia, Colombia, Ecuador and Peru.

The Russians, moreover, have learnt to respect the self-righteous persistence of the Chinese and must be uneasily aware of the long-term factors Peking might exploit in the Latin American and Caribbean region: the Chinese communities in Peru and Ecuador, for instance, or the poverty-stricken peasantry of Mexico and the Andean countries who, in Chinese eyes, have a double virtue in that they are not only peasants but Indians with whom the Chinese can, and do, claim ethnic affinity. (Perhaps this was why, in July 1965, Moscow radio started broadcasting in the Andean Quechua tongue, calling on the Indians to overthrow their oppressors and restore the Inca empire.)

It was not enough to condemn dissident groups, such as the Communist Party of Brazil, as Moscow did by radio and printed word, in such publications as the *World Marxist Review*. A more convincing demonstration of unity within the Moscow fold was needed and the Russians supplied the need in November 1964 by calling a conference of all Latin American Communist parties in Havana. There was understandably a certain secrecy about the staging of this important event, partly because a number of parties were illegal and travel arrangements for representatives had to be clandestine; and partly, no doubt, because Moscow might not have wished to reveal that a conference had taken place at all if the delegates had been unwilling to toe the Soviet line. The fact that there had been a conference was not, in fact, published until January 18, 1965, when Tass reported that the delegates had met at the end of 1964, but without saying where. Western observers jumped rather readily to the conclusion that it must have been held somewhere in eastern Europe, on the ground that it could not have been kept dark for so long if held in a presumably talkative Latin American country. It was learnt later however that the place was Havana—less talkative, perhaps, than it had been before communism became entrenched there. In one respect, though, western guesses had been close to the mark, for the delegates, or most of them, had travelled to Havana by way of *Prague* (yet another example of that capital's subversive role in Moscow's interests).

There are two other interesting things to note about the Havana conference. One is that the Latin American parties subscribed to Moscow's ideological line; the other, that Moscow, tacitly subscribed to Fidel Castro's line of violent insurrection. It was all in the communiqué, for those acquainted with the jargon. 'Fractions' were condemned. Translated into plain English, this referred to pro-Chinese or Trotskyist groups that had sprung up among Latin American Communists. By implication, this was a criticism of Cuba, which had supported certain Trotskyist groups, as well as of China. Cuba, however, was given a promise of support, and the communiqué called for 'active aid' to the 'freedom fighters in Venezuela, Colombia, Guatemala, Honduras, Paraguay and Haiti'. This was a reaffirmation, in Latin American terms, of Moscow's pledge, under the 1960 Declaration, to help 'national liberation movements' everywhere, and was intended to cut the ground from under the feet of the nasty Chinese, who had been telling everybody the Russians weren't serious about national liberation.

The disgruntled Chinese invited Che Guevara of Cuba to Peking to explain what it was all about. This was *one* meeting that ended without an agreed statement. And the Chinese press kept quiet about the Cubans' visit, apart from reporting the bare facts. But soon enough the world knew what the Chinese really thought of Havana, through that habitual mouthpiece or kite-flyer of the Chinese Communists, the Albanian party paper, *Zeri i Popullit*, which, on February 16—a week after the Cubans had left Peking—described the conference as a confidence trick of Moscow's to exploit Cuba's prestige as a true revolutionary. For good measure, the Albanians referred to the devilish cunning of the revisionists (read 'Russians'), and their diabolical schemes.

The struggle for the Third World went on.

2

Fidel Unveiled

ON DECEMBER 2, 1961, Fidel Castro vindicated Soviet faith in 'national democracy' by publicly declaring that he had been a Marxist for years. Not much of a Marxist, he admitted, since he had never managed to read beyond page 370 of *Das Kapital*; but he promised he was going to make up for lost time, for now at last he was a true revolutionary.

A year before, when the world's communists were meeting in Moscow, Schools of Revolutionary Instruction had been set up in Cuba and at the end of January 1962, Castro told *Pravda* and *Isvestiya* that 20,000 party members had graduated there in Marxism-Leninism (and, it appears, in Maoism, an aspect that cannot have pleased the Russians). What party did Castro mean? He was referring, in fact, to an achievement in which he took special pride—a kind of diploma of his revolutionary graduation—the creation of the United Socialist Revolutionary Party.

The PURS, as it is known from its initials in Spanish, superseded the Integrated Revolutionary Organisations, which themselves merged three groups: the Cuban Communist Party (known as the PSP or Popular Socialist Party), the March 13 Revolutionary Directorate and Fidel Castro's own July 26 Movement (referring to the date of the abortive revolt he launched in 1953). What this meant was soon apparent when leading communists were appointed to key jobs in the PURS and the government.*

It is not my purpose to trace the course of Cuba's communisation and of its satellisation by the Soviet Union. Two points, however, need to be grasped: Cuba under Castro did

* On October 3, 1965, the PURS was reorganised on orthodox Moscow lines to become the Cuban Communist Party.

'go communist', and it rapidly came to be economically dependent on the Soviet bloc. On November 11, 1962, the Cuban communist paper, *Hoy*, disclosed that the Soviet Union had provided Cuba with more than £303 million in economic aid since the two countries signed their first trade agreement in February 1960. During that time, the annual value of Russo-Cuban trade had soared from £30 million to £130 million.

The *Hoy* figures did not, however, include the value of Soviet military deliveries. If these are added, together with the value of invisible (and perhaps unmentionable) services, it may well be concluded that Cuba, without Russian aid, would hardly be in a position to sustain its costly and evidently long-term campaigns of subversion in other places, which include Africa and the English and French-speaking Caribbean as well as continental Latin America and the Dominican Republic.

Nor is this all: many millions more must be added to the large figures already mentioned to cover the value of aid from Poland and Hungary, Czechoslovakia and Rumania, and Bulgaria and East Germany. And one or more of these collaborated with Cuba in special subversive operations, notably in Zanzibar in December 1963 and in the Dominican Republic in April 1965.

Cuban subversion is indeed what does concern us here. Every other country in Latin America has come in for its share of it—in itself an index of the ambitious scale of the whole operation and of its high financial cost. Although Cuban spokesmen have denied it, the export of revolution is indeed a central aim of Cuba's foreign policy, as the public declarations of Fidel Castro and Che Guevara showed beyond surmise. As early as 1959, Cuban-organised forces set sail on abortive invasion expeditions against the Dominican Republic, Haiti, Nicaragua and Panama. But this was before Castro had learnt his Marxism-Leninism. Once he had become a 'true revolutionary', there was to be no more tilting at windmills. The export of revolution was to be put on a professional basis.

Overtly the first sign of the line was the Second Declaration of Havana, which Castro read publicly in February 1962, and which called on the Latin American peoples to overthrow their governments. But by this time, Castro's agents were already at work in most, if not all, of the countries of continental Latin America: this was the new professionalism.

Fidel Castro was still Quixotic enough, on the other hand, to expect quick results, and on January 16, 1963, he expressed his bitterness at the timidity of Latin American revolutionaries —more specifically at the rejection of his policy by local Communist parties. When July 26—the anniversary of his own movement—came round, however, he issued a second revolutionary appeal to the peoples of Latin America. 'In many Latin American countries', he declared, 'revolutionary conditions are incomparably better than they were in our country.'

If Castro was the orator of this policy of interference, Guevara was its theoretician and executant. Guevara had been one of Castro's most successful guerrilla commanders in the field, and in 1959 he theorised from his experience in a book published the following year under the title *La Guerra de Guerrillas* ('Guerrilla Warfare'). Guevara borrowed a little from Mao but not at all from the Russians. His little book, which has become the basic text for Fidelista revolutionaries throughout the area, is, in fact, rather heretical. It puts up Cuba as the revolutionary model, denies any special mission for the proletariat (in this respect going even further than Mao does) and argues—against Lenin and his followers—that revolutionaries needn't wait for the right 'objective' conditions to launch their revolution, since the mere fact of going into insurrection will create such conditions.

This is Guevara the theoretician. But he, too, is capable of oratory. And on May Day 1962, he declared that the popular masses of Latin America were only waiting for a signal—from Cuba, it appeared—to 'hurl themselves into the struggle to take over power by any means'.

There has, in fact, been no shortage of 'signals': I have just cited several. More important than oratory or theory, however, are evidences of actual interference in other countries. We have seen that Cuba exports revolution as far afield as Africa. But its Latin American effort is naturally far more extensive. Castro's agents have been indefatigable in the recruitment of young revolutionaries in neighbouring countries. Much of the evidence has come from Cuban refugees and deserters, whose stories have been crosschecked. Already in 1961, according to an early and detailed report, students from Argentina, Brazil, Chile, Ecuador and Guatemala were following courses of Marxist-Leninist propaganda techniques in Havana. The young men—aged 16 to 20—were sent on to the Minas del Frío training centre in Oriente province, where they were taught how to use small arms. Intensive courses were also being run as early as 1961 at Las Arenas, also in Oriente, where trainees were instructed in sabotage and guerrilla tactics, subversion and propaganda. By now, the number of trainees who have followed these courses must run into thousands, for there has been a continuous intake of new batches at intervals of eight weeks.

Fidel Castro's revolutionary factories have yielded a growing output of political violence and murder, of which the most striking example is in Venezuela. Like Cuba, Venezuela had endured a militarist dictatorship and overthrown it. But Castro had overthrown Batista's right-wing tyranny only to lead Cuba to a tyranny of the Left. In Venezuela, tyranny itself had been removed and the constitutional rule of President Betancourt and his Acción Democrática (AD) party had replaced the arbitrary reign of the deposed Pérez-Jiménez. This, perhaps, above all was what Fidel Castro found intolerable in Venezuela.

The direct originator of left-wing violence was the MIR (from the Spanish initials of 'Left Revolutionary Movement'), a strongly Fidelista offshoot of the ruling AD Party. The MIR was formed in 1960, not long after Castro's victory in Cuba but before he had declared himself to be a communist. Later the MIR combined with what was then the leading opposition party, the URD ('Democratic Republican Union') and the Venezuelan Communist Party to form the National Liberation Front (FLN)—the political organ behind the terrorists and guerrillas. At that time, the Communist Party, though ostensibly pro-Soviet, was divided on the issue of violence.

The apostles of violence, however, were already in the ascendant at the Third Congress of the party in March 1961, and definitely gained the day in December 1962, when the Central Committee called for the formation of 'a popular army grouping all Venezuelan patriots' to overthrow Betancourt. Shortly afterwards, the 'patriots' of the FLN formed a militant arm, the Armed Forces of National Liberation (FALN), which grouped together both the urban terrorists who for some time had been throwing bombs in Caracas, and incipient guerrilla groups in the mountains of western Venezuela.

Though the FALN is not exclusively Fidelista, the evidence that its terrorists and guerrilla fighters were trained in Cuba and that its arms came from there is overwhelming. The discovery in November 1963 of three tons of arms of Cuban origin at a remote place on the Paraguana Peninsula was drawn to the attention of the Organisation of American States (OAS), which until then had been reluctant to condemn Cuba as unequivocally as the United States might have wished. A five-man OAS mission later found that Venezuela

> . . . has been the target of a series of actions, sponsored and directed by the government of Cuba, openly intended to subvert Venezuelan institutions and to overthrow the democratic government of Venezuela through terrorism, sabotage and guerrilla warfare.

The climax of the Cuban-sponsored assault on Venezuela was to have come on December 1, 1963. On that day, Venezuelans were to go to the polls to elect a new President. This was the experiment which was to be made to fail, and the communists called on voters to boycott the election. To drive the point home, they intensified both terrorism in the cities and guerrilla activity in the countryside. The idea was not the relatively simple one of overthrowing Betancourt and taking power, for the communists were aware that they were too weak, and the armed forces too strong, for that to happen. Their aim was the more Macchiavellian one of unnerving Betancourt and forcing him to hand over power to a military junta. The FLN reckoned that in that event they could repeat Castro's defeat of Batista's armed forces by provoking a disintegration of the Venezuelan military.

To Betancourt's enduring credit, this did not happen. True, he did waver for a while, but his great achievement was not only to have pulled himself together, but to have persuaded the armed forces to restore law and order *without* seizing power for themselves. On the appointed day, 90 per cent of the voters defied the communists and voted.

After this crushing defeat, the communists and Fidelistas were relatively quiet for some months, but by the time these lines were written—late in 1965—violence was surging up again, especially in the countryside. Early in the year, the FALN had published a military plan for 1965, calling for closer coordination of the guerrilla fronts in various States. Bribery and terrorism on a mounting scale were being used to recruit guerrilla fighters among the peasants. Money stolen from shops, banks and factories was being spent to buy food at inflated prices from the local population. Such practical bribes were supplemented by promises of land, directed especially at those peasants who had not yet benefited from the government's own land reform scheme. For recalcitrant peasants, torture and exemplary murders were the next stages of the recruiting campaign.

The Fidelista MIR remained the pace-setter in revolutionary violence, but the orthodox, Moscow-line Venezuelan Communist Party was not far behind, for one of its leaders, Eduardo Gallegos Mancera, declared on a visit to Czechoslovakia that 'armed struggle is the most important, though not the only, form of revolutionary struggle'. Once again, indeed, when it comes to subversion and violence, one finds communists of overtly diverging views lining up in the same side of the fence. When the FALN opened a new international centre in Havana on November 14, 1964, for instance, three ambassadors turned up: they represented the Soviet Union, China and North Vietnam. And the following April, an Italian and Argentino—both communists—were arrested on entering Venezuela carrying well over £100,000 in dollar notes, allegedly to finance the Venezuelan Communist Party's subversive efforts.

The Venezuelan example is reproduced, with variations, in other Latin American countries. In November and December 1962, for instance, the Peruvian Trotskyist, Hugo Blanco, with Cuban support, launched a terrorist campaign which, however, ended with his arrest and that of most of his followers. The communists were no more discouraged by this failure than later by the Venezuelan one. June 1965 brought a fresh wave of violence, in the Andes east of Lima. As in Venezuela the terrorists took their orders from a body calling itself the Left Revolutionary Movement (MIR). One of their leaders, Guillermo Lobaton Mille, had been trained in Cuba and China; and another, Ismael Parades, in Cuba and Czechoslovakia. Under their orders, Peruvian Indian bands were committing murders, attacking haciendas and blowing up bridges.

In Colombia, the Cubans associated themselves with long-established bandits under the leadership of one Pedro Antonio Marín, better known as 'Dead Shot' (Tiro Fijo), who is credited with 800 murders. According to the Bogota daily, *La República* —a moderate sheet—Tiro Fijo and his closest associates are members of the central committee of the Colombian Communist Party. This may explain why the Soviet periodical *New Times* has carried an article praising rebel activities in Colombia. But the Chinese and Cuban newspapers, too, praise the Colombian outlaws, for this, as we have seen, is where the brotherhood of subversion takes over from ideological dissension.

For temperamental and emotional reasons, the Cuban and Chinese communists feel particularly close to bandits or guerrillas fighting in the name of the peasantry. It is not by coincidence that Prestes and the official Brazilian Communist Party stayed aloof from the leader of the so-called Peasant Leagues of north-eastern Brazil, Francisco Julião, whereas the Chinese and Cubans received him with open arms. This, however, was in 1961 and 1962, when communist infiltration under the complacent President Goulart seemed to be proving the Russians right in their 'model' for revolution. The truth is that Moscow will stay silent about 'national liberation' insurrections when they fail (as in Venezuela at the end of 1963) and praise them when they start having successes.

Certainly the Russians do nothing to dissociate themselves from, much less to hinder, Cuban subversion, one of the most striking instances of which took place during the confused days of the uprising by followers of ex-President Juan Bosch in the Dominican Republic in April, 1965. For months, Dominican communists of varying shades, trained in the arts of sabotage, terrorism and guerrilla warfare, had been smuggled back into the republic from various countries, including Cuba and Czechoslovakia. Some belonged to the Dominican Popular Socialist Party (the orthodox Moscow-line Communist party); others were members of two still more violent Fidelista groups, the Popular Dominican Movement and the June 14 Movement.

These men had well-indoctrinated friends among junior Army officers; and when it looked as though Bosch's followers were facing defeat at the hands of the military, the communists used their own military contacts to gain access to the arsenals. Within hours they had distributed arms to hundreds of well-prepared civilians. There is no doubt that at this stage—about April 28—the original democratic movement for the return of Juan Bosch passed out of the control of the democrats and into the hands of the communists. Simultaneously, the anti-Bosch forces, under General Wessin y Wessin, started disintegrating as the indoctrinated junior officers changed sides. It was at this stage that President Johnson ordered the marines to land in Santo Domingo.

The American intervention naturally aroused widespread indignation, not only among communists, but also among many well-intentioned liberals and socialists. It is not part of my purpose to defend the manner in which President Johnson conducted his intervention or presented his case to the world. But I am convinced, on the evidence, that if he had not intervened, the Dominican Republic would by now have been another Cuba. Many estimable correspondents and commentators flatly deny this possibility and see only the obvious damage the intervention did to America's peace-loving image, the supposed blow it dealt to Dominican 'democracy' and the resentment it undoubtedly aroused among Latin Americans. It is their right to be indignant. But I found their naivety surprising and disturbing.

The American Central Intelligence Agency had published a list of 58 (later reduced to 55) communist ringleaders who had taken over the pro-Bosch insurrection. Many of the 156 correspondents who flocked to Santo Domingo to cover the story expressed surprise that these men were not to be found. Did they really suppose the communists would hang around to be interviewed after the Americans had intervened, thereby proving President Johnson right? Surprise and scepticism were also expressed among the newspapermen because they could not find any evidence of communist sympathies among the ordinary followers of Colonel Caamaño, the military leader of the pro-Bosch insurgents, and because even the CIA had been able to name only fifty or sixty communists. But since when have communists needed to be in a majority to gain control of a revolution? Had the marines not landed, the communists would have been seen all right; for in that event, they would have been in power.

There is, however, no need for a Dominican hypothesis to show what Fidel Castro's agents are up to in Latin America.

What I have done in this chapter is to assemble only the barest facts of a conspiracy that extends, in one form or another, throughout the Latin American and Caribbean areas.

V

The Threat
in Perspective

I

The Threat in Perspective

WHEN THE late Senator Joseph McCarthy was witchhunting in the 1950s, no American whose views were a millimetre left of centre could sleep soundly in his bed. Today eminent American intellectuals, such as Professors Kennan and Morgenthau, are preaching a new form of appeasement and isolationism for which, in McCarthy's day, they would have been hounded to distraction. And the curious marathon seminar called the 'teach-in' has crossed the Atlantic to become a handy device for berating the United States. 'The progressive syndrome', Constantine FitzGibbon has called it.

When Chamberlain was appeasing Hitler, the progressives were indignant. Today, they would like President Johnson to appease Mao, Ho, Brezhnev and Castro. Totalitarianism must, it seems, be stopped when it is of the right, and allowed to prevail when it comes from the left.

Let us avoid the twin pitfalls of professional anti-communism and 'progressivism'. The former tends to claim that nothing has changed in the world communist movement; and the latter to declare that the communist threat—to the extent that there ever was such a thing—has vanished along with the world movement. Either view is simplistic. There is still an international communist threat, but it is untidier and more complicated than it used to be. The evidence collected in this book confirms beyond doubt, I think, the persistence of the threat. Indeed in the Third World there are strong grounds for saying that the new phenomenon of competitive subversion has intensified the threat.

Let us not, however, lose our sense of perspective. The Third World, though overwhelming in terms of population and area, is not the *whole* world; nor is competitive subversion the only aspect of communism.

From the standpoint of the 'capitalist' countries of the West, the communist threat is nothing like as grave as it was in the aggressive post-war Stalinist phase, when the Soviet armies threatened western Europe, when Mao Tse-tung's victory extended the area of the communist monolith over two-thirds of the Euro-Asian land mass and the workers of Italy and France were ready to strike or riot at Moscow's orders.

Today the monolith has cracked and a deepening chasm of hostility separates Moscow from Peking. When Moscow cracks the whip, the wild beasts no longer perform the required motions. The Russians tried to call a world communist conference in 1964, at which the Chinese party was to be made to toe the line or be drummed out of the world movement. But the response was so poor that the conference could not be held until March 1965; and when it was, it had to be re-labelled as a mere consultative gathering, which only nineteen parties, including the Soviet, attended. In France, though the Communist Party still attracts a massive protest vote, membership has declined drastically, and the party no longer seems able to call riots at will. The smaller western Communist parties are confused, incoherent and demoralised. Even communist eastern Europe is no longer monolithically responsive to Moscow's orders. The Rumanians, especially, go their own way, to the extent of refusing to send a delegation to the Moscow conference in March 1965.

All this is true, but it is only part of the truth. We have seen that when it is a question of destroying or undermining the emerging countries, doctrinal differences between Peking and Moscow, or between Belgrade and Havana, really matter very little. Nor does the fact that the Rumanians are recalcitrant. To the American and South Vietnamese soldiers fighting the Viet Cong, or to the ordinary people of Venezuela under terrorist attacks, the fact that ideology and tactics are in dispute in international communist gatherings is of academic interest.

To them, what matters is the hard reality of the fight for survival. And although it has now become apparently impossible for the Chinese and the Russians jointly to draft and sign a document, the agents of Peking, Moscow and Havana happen to be working for common aims, which include the subversion of vulnerable regimes in the new countries, if these are considered insufficiently revolutionary.

It cannot even be said that the cracking of the monolith has been uniformly harmful to individual Communist parties. Certainly it has seriously damaged the smaller parties. But the late Palmiro Togliatti, leader of the large Italian Communist Party, was shrewd enough to see that what he called 'polycentrism' could actually benefit his own party. 'Polycentrism' was the term he coined in 1956 to describe the phenomenon of 'different roads to socialism' which Khrushchev had sanctioned in his speeches at the Twentieth Congress of the Soviet party in February that year.

What Togliatti perceived was that a mass party like the Italian could use 'polycentrism' to strengthen its claim to be a truly national party, independent of any control from Moscow or Peking. It is interesting to note in this connection that the Italian party has continued to improve on the percentage of votes it has attracted through successive elections.

Polycentrism must be accounted at least a factor in this slow but steady advance (although to see the picture in perspective, one must remember that the Italian Communist Party is much weaker now than it was immediately after the Second World War). Some observers believe that the party's performance in 1965 shows it has suffered from the death of Togliatti. This may be true, but it does not affect the argument. At the very least, one may say that polycentrism has not been a handicap to the Italian communists. And we have seen that the same has been true, in even greater degree, of the Indonesian communists—another mass party with national pretensions.

All things considered, then, the theory that the disintegration of the world communist movement, as Stalin knew it, has removed the communist threat, does not stand up to the evidence.

There are, however, several complementary theories, which appeal, for one reason or another, to people who cannot be considered 'progressive' (in the pejorative sense) or in any way fellow-travellers. One theory is that the Russians have become 'fat' and unaggressive, and I have produced evidence that demolishes it in various parts of this book. Another theory is that China—whether ruled by communists or others—is fundamentally pacific. To deal with this one in detail would take me well beyond the scope of this study. But one thing can be said: the overwhelming evidence of Chinese subversion in countries far beyond its borders is alone sufficient to disprove the theory.

A further theory might be termed anticipatory and philosophical. It rests on the argument that the *character* of communism is changing, especially in Russia and other east European countries, so that within a generation or so communism will no longer be the menacing thing that it has been. In one sense, this is a variant of the 'fat communists' theory; but it has a Chinese application for, it is argued, the Chinese are incurable individualists, traders and capitalists so that, no matter what the Chinese Communist Party does, communism cannot survive in China.

Let met say at once that, although I am not a historical determinist, I don't reject this theory out of hand. I fear, however, that very little legitimate consolation may be derived from it. Communism is indeed constantly changing its character, in the sense that revisionism is a permanent feature of Marxism-Leninism. Even the Chinese communists, those determined defenders of doctrinal purity, were more revisionist than the Russians have been before or since, in 1956 and 1957 when Mao Tse-tung was allowing the expression of dissenting opinion during the curious episode known as the Hundred Flowers ('Let one hundred flowers bloom, one hundred schools of thought contend') and was claiming that China's 'people's communes' would bring full communism to China in one easy stage.

Ideology in itself, however, is of less interest than the use that is made of it. The important thing is that Communist parties are in power in fourteen countries. Not only are they in power but their claim to a monopoly of power rests on a doctrine that justifies the overthrow of all non-communist systems. It has always seemed to me extremely unlikely that any ruling Communist Party, however 'revisionist', would ever undermine its own monopoly of power by calling in question a fundamental point of doctrine, such as the class struggle (which, as we have seen in my first chapter, has an international as well as an internal validity). Should this ever happen, there would indeed no longer be a communist problem as we know it. But it seems far more probable that individual ruling Communist parties will be overthrown long before this point is reached. This, after all, was what very nearly happened in Hungary in 1956; and I don't think one can rule out the possibility that it will happen in time in the Soviet Union itself.

If it does, it will be less a revolt against tyranny (as in Hungary) than a revulsion against the fundamental inefficiency of the system and its apparent incapacity to resolve its own policy dilemmas. One of these we have considered in various chapters: the contradiction between the State policy of understanding with the United States and the party policy of support for subversion. But there are other contradictions. One is the inability of the Soviet economic system simultaneously to catch up with American living standards, maintain a huge defence establishment *and* compete with the United States in the space race.

In agriculture, the communist system has been a disastrous failure in the Soviet Union and other communist countries. In industry, there have been great successes, notably in steel production and science. But you can neither eat steel nor wear it, and the glut of unwanted and unsold goods in the State shops has led to the partial adoption of some apparently heretical theories of the Soviet economist, Professor Liberman, who advocates profitability as an index of industrial efficiency and wants production of consumer goods to be geared to the needs of the consumer, not the fantasies of the planners.

These developments and the evidence of increasing scepticism and inquisitiveness on the part of students and writers have led some observers to conclude that Russia is returning to capitalism and dreaming of introducing democracy. In the long term, I agree, such developments, if carried to their logical conclusions, would challenge the bases of the communist monopoly of power. But to suppose that the logical conclusions are round the corner would be to fly in the face of the facts. Russia is *not* returning to capitalism, and the simplest disproof of the contention is the fact that people who practise private enterprise can be shot for it.

In May 1961, at the height of Khrushchev's 'revisionism', the death penalty was extended for a number of economic 'crimes'. Some of the offences for which Soviet citizens have been executed in larger numbers than outsiders realise are crimes in non-communist States. But many people have been shot during the past few years simply for producing and selling, for private profit, goods in short supply because of the inefficiency of State-controlled enterprise. To pick an example at random, five men were shot, according to the Soviet press, in February 1963, for illegally manufacturing and selling fountain pens, rulers and other small but useful objects.

Nor, of course, is the Soviet government in the least likely to ask students and writers who ask awkward questions to form a legal opposition party. The Soviet Union remains a totalitarian State.

How nice it would be, to be sure, if the Russians abandoned subversion as an instrument of policy. We must beware, however, of those who advocate western economic aid for the Soviet Union on the ground that this will 'fatten' the Russians quicker and make them less dangerous. On this issue at least, the 'progressives' are not alone, especially in Britain, for many businessmen, politicians and civil servants either accept this view or argue that Britain's need for export markets overrides any possible harm that could result from, say, giving Russia exceptionally favourable credit terms.

For my part, I cannot accept such arguments. I cannot see why Britain or other Western countries should help to remove the economic limitations on the free exercise of Soviet foreign policy. Two things, in particular, would dramatically increase the Soviet Union's capacity to wage a successful cold war: a substantial reduction in its arms burden and an effective chemical and technological revolution on the land. To help the Russians achieve the second of these aims would enable the Soviet Communist Party to claim a success in agriculture which it has entirely failed to achieve by the application of Marxist-Leninist theories. As for disarmament, it will come, if it does, as a consequence of reduced tensions and abandoned policies; it will not precede such changes. In the present state of the world communist movement, should the German question be miraculously solved and disarmament achieved, one of the predictable consequences would be a feverish rise in Moscow's subversive efforts in the Third World. Moreover, success on the land and a reduced arms burden would improve Russia's capacity to support distant communist regimes, such as Cuba's.

It will be time enough to help Russia when the country's rulers have abandoned subversion. After all, there is nothing to stop them giving it up, except doctrine and the fear of losing all control over the world's Communist parties to the more militant Chinese. As things stand, Russia remains a greater menace than China (despite China's recent acquisition of a nuclear weapon) because Russia is richer and stronger.

The fanaticism and persistence of the Chinese Communist Party, on the other hand, present increasing dangers to the rest of the world. Nor is there any discernible prospect that the character of Chinese communism will change. True, the Chinese press itself has often complained of the inveterate tendency of the Chinese to revert to capitalism. True again, Mao Tse-tung and his companions are old men, who must soon yield power to younger leaders who may reject the intransigence of their elders. True again, even Mao did give dissidents a say in 1957.

The Chinese Communist Party is, indeed, aware of the question-marks such issues raise for the future of communism in China. But the existence of doubts is admitted only the better to suppress them. The 'Hundred Flowers' were killed in a wave of fresh repression of the intellectuals. The inveterate capitalism of the Chinese is mentioned only so that it may be castigated. As for the party's monopoly of power, the present leaders intend to preserve it not merely in our lifetimes but for generations. The euphoric optimism of the 'great leap forward' in 1958 has gone. In November that year, the most ancient of the party leaders, Marshal Chu Teh, had exclaimed:

> The world of universal harmony of which mankind has dreamt for thousands of years, the communist society for which communists have striven for over 100 years, will be brought into being by your own generation and by your own hands.

The nagging fear that future Chinese leaders may forsake communism is now uppermost. China's Young Communist League devoted an entire session in June and July 1964 to the problem of training future leaders who would stick to communism. The first secretary of the League, Hu Yao-pang, declared that the transitional period to communism would take 'five to ten—or even more—generations'.

Perhaps the fears of the Chinese leaders will prove well founded and China will indeed abandon communism. But the gloomy fanaticism that can envisage ten or more generations of struggle should not be underestimated. For the outside world, the communist problem will last at least as long as communist rule persists in China. The struggle for the Third World will be a protracted one.